To the Called

BISHOP STANLEY CHOATE

TO THE CALLED

BISHOP
STANLEY
CHOATE

Belleville, Ontario, Canada

To the Called

ISBN: 978-1-4600-0947-5
LSI Edition: 978-1-4600-0948-2
E-book ISBN: 978-1-4600-0949-9
(E-book available from the Kindle Store, KOBO and the iBooks Store)

To order additional copies, visit:
www.essencebookstore.com

For more information, please contact:

New England Pentecostal Ministries
955 Bridge St
Pelham, NH 03076 USA
NEPMinistries@gmail.com

Guardian Books is an imprint of *Essence Publishing,* a Christian Book Publisher dedicated to furthering the work of Christ through the written word. For more information, contact:

20 Hanna Court, Belleville, Ontario, Canada K8P 5J2
Phone: 1-800-238-6376 • Fax: (613) 962-3055
Email: info@essence-publishing.com
Web site: www.essence-publishing.com

CONTENTS

FOREWORD

For some time, God has been dealing with me about writing another book on the affairs of the church.

From day one of my salvation, the Spirit has placed in me a deep concern for the church. I know that the church is supposed to do a mighty work in the last days and that these are the last days, but as I look at the condition of the church and how we are so separated, I wonder how the work will be accomplished. Therefore, I always pray for the church and repent for her sins, hoping to see us unified to fulfill God's mission.

Now I'm here, attempting to do my little part and address the issues of the church. This book is designed by the spirit to make us aware of the heart of God. His heart is broken by the condition of His church—the one that He has invested so much into, even His own blood, and now He sees His church in disarray and it is disheartening.

I believe this message is given to others around the world. The call is going out. It's now our time. We must be about our Father's business. This book is directed *To the Called.*

As you read through this book, you will see that some scriptures are repeated to make a different point, so the redundancy is not without purpose. This book may also serve well in a Bible study setting.

Ready, let's go!

Bishop Stanley O. Choate

The Called

CHAPTER ONE

As I sit here at my desk on a Friday afternoon wondering how to begin this book, I believe the Lord has given me the name of the book, *To the Called,* so that is where I will begin.

The Bible states that many are called but only a few are chosen (Matthew 20:16). It is easy to raise one's hand to say, "I have been called of the Lord"; there is a second part of that scripture, however, that bears restating: only a few are chosen.

So, to the called, the time is now. The work is at hand. The question is, will you be chosen?

We, the church, have been called out of the world and chosen by God to be His body, His ambassador, and to speak for Him.

> *Therefore if any man be in Christ, he is a new creature: old things are passed away; behold, all things are become new. And all things are of God, who hath reconciled us to himself by Jesus Christ, and hath given to us the ministry of reconciliation; To wit, that God was in Christ, reconciling the world unto himself, not imputing their*

trespasses unto them; and hath committed unto us the word of reconciliation. Now then we are ambassadors for Christ, as though God did beseech you by us: we pray you in Christ's stead, be ye reconciled to God. For he hath made him to be sin for us, who knew no sin; that we might be made the righteousness of God in him (2 Corinthians 5:17-21).

We have been called into the kingdom of God for such a time as this—a time when great darkness fills the earth. Now it's time for us to be the light. We are called to do the work of the kingdom, as a coworker with Christ, as we are joint heirs.

For as many as are led by the Spirit of God, they are the sons of God. For ye have not received the spirit of bondage again to fear; but ye have received the Spirit of adoption, whereby we cry, Abba, Father. The Spirit itself beareth witness with our spirit, that we are the children of God: And if children, then heirs; heirs of God, and joint-heirs with Christ; if so be that we suffer with him, that we may be also glorified together (Romans 8:14-17).

We are called to be the full measure and stature of Christ in the earth, with kingdom power and authority.

And he gave some, apostles; and some, prophets; and some, evangelists; and some, pastors and teachers; For the perfecting of the saints, for the work of the ministry, for the edifying of the body of Christ: Till we all come in the unity of the faith, and of the knowledge of the Son of God, unto a perfect man, unto the measure of the stature of the fulness of Christ: That we henceforth be no more children, tossed to and fro, and carried about with every wind of doctrine, by the sleight of men, and cunning craftiness, whereby they lie in wait to deceive; But speaking the truth in love, may grow up into him in all things, which is the head, even Christ: From whom the whole body fitly joined together and compacted by that which every joint supplieth, according to the effectual working in the measure of every part, maketh increase of the body unto the edifying of itself in love (Ephesians 4:11-16).

How can we emerge into all these things He has called us to be if we are not willing to become one? As a single member of the body, we can never become the fullness of Christ. This can only happen by us working together as one.

We are living in a time where many pastors and church members don't realize that there is only one body, of which we are all part. If we ever hope to fulfill our purpose, we must be as one. The call is to the body, not to individual members. Do you understand that life and purpose can only be found in the body?

Therefore, the call is going out:

Arise, My church, cast off your slumber, for the day of your purpose has come—the day I have chosen before the foundation of the world, that you would stand in these last days and represent Me in the earth.

To the called, humble yourselves and make yourself ready for what I am going to do through you.

To the called, I say come unto Me that I may renew you in Me. Purify and sanctify yourselves unto Me, for the work is great.

As you can see, God is calling upon us to come together and take a stand in these last days. This is a time when wickedness is great in the earth, and many souls are being lost as a result of it. Are we going to continue to stand by while souls are being lost, knowing that we can help? If we present ourselves unto the Lord, He will equip us for the work.

I hear the Lord saying that He has not called us because we are great in number, but few, that His glory might be revealed. It's time to work.

The work has been identified by the signs. 2 Timothy 3:1-5 says that the people would have a "form of godliness" yet deny the transforming power of the Holy Ghost. We have been instructed not to associate with such people.

In this context, the word *form* means that something has an appearance of truth but is not true in nature. The book of Jude goes even further, declaring in verses 3-7 and 17-21 these words:

> *Beloved, when I gave all diligence to write unto you of the common salvation, it was needful for me to write unto you, and exhort you that ye should earnestly contend for the faith which was once delivered unto the saints. For there are certain men crept in unawares, who were before of old ordained to this condemnation, ungodly men, turning the grace of our God into lasciviousness, and denying the only Lord God, and our Lord Jesus Christ. I will therefore put you in remembrance, though ye once knew this, how that the Lord, having saved the people out of the land of Egypt, afterward destroyed them that believed not. And the angels which kept not their first estate, but left their own habitation, he hath reserved in everlasting chains under darkness unto the judgment of the great day. Even as Sodom and Gomorrha, and the cities about them in like manner,*

> *giving themselves over to fornication, and going after strange flesh, are set forth for an example, suffering the vengeance of eternal fire.*
>
> *But, beloved, remember ye the words which were spoken before of the apostles of our Lord Jesus Christ; How that they told you there should be mockers in the last time, who should walk after their own ungodly lusts. These be they who separate themselves, sensual, having not the Spirit. But ye, beloved, building up yourselves on your most holy faith, praying in the Holy Ghost, Keep yourselves in the love of God, looking for the mercy of our Lord Jesus Christ unto eternal life.*

Even though all this was occurring, Jude assured them that they could be kept during this time:

> *Now unto him that is able to keep you from falling, and to present you faultless before the presence of his glory with exceeding joy, To the only wise God our Saviour, be glory and majesty, dominion and power, both now and ever. Amen* (Jude 24-25).

Jude also admonished them to build themselves up in their most holy faith. So, we are to build ourselves up in our most holy faith.

However, most have become complacent and even lazy, for they have lost their zeal for the things of God. As the church becomes weaker, the darkness has gotten greater.

To the called, the good thing is that the work is the Lord's and whatever He starts, no matter how impossible it seems, He will complete it. Because we are the vessels, all the glory goes to God.

> *Then the word of the Lord came unto me, saying, Before I formed thee in the belly I knew thee; and before thou camest forth out of the womb I sanctified thee, and I ordained thee a prophet unto the nations. Then said I, Ah, Lord God! behold, I cannot speak: for I am a child. But the Lord said unto me, Say not, I am a child: for thou shalt go to all that I shall send thee, and whatsoever I command thee thou shalt speak. Be not afraid of their faces: for I am with thee to deliver thee, saith the Lord. Then the Lord put forth his hand, and touched my mouth. And the Lord said unto me, Behold, I have put my words in thy mouth. See, I have this day set thee over the nations and over the kingdoms, to root out, and to pull down, and to destroy, and to throw down, to build, and to plant* (Jeremiah 1:4-10).

These verses show us the things that Jeremiah had to deal with. This condition is true of the people of God today. It is sad to say, but these were the people of God, the ones that He had chosen.

Lost in the House

CHAPTER TWO

Just because God has called us does not mean that we can sit back and do nothing. There is a charge to keep.

Let's look at Matthew 3:1-3:

In those days came John the Baptist, preaching in the wilderness of Judaea, And saying, Repent ye: for the kingdom of heaven is at hand. For this is he that was spoken of by the prophet Esaias, saying, The voice of one crying in the wilderness, Prepare ye the way of the Lord, make his paths straight.

This is what he said in verses 7 and 8:

But when he saw many of the Pharisees and Sadducees come to his baptism, he said unto them, O generation of vipers, who hath warned you to flee from the wrath to come? Bring forth therefore fruits meet for repentance.

He was requiring fruit of them, but they did not see the need for repentance. So, this is what was said in verse 9:

And think not to say within yourselves, We have Abraham to our father: for I say unto you, that God is able of these stones to raise up children unto Abraham.

Because of the ungodliness of God's people, we find in 1 Kings 17 that God raised up the prophet Elijah to speak to the people. In 1 Kings 18:20-21, God spoke through Elijah:

> *So Ahab sent unto all the children of Israel, and gathered the prophets together unto mount Carmel. And Elijah came unto all the people, and said, How long halt ye between two opinions? if the Lord be God, follow him: but if Baal, then follow him. And the people answered him not a word.*

Again, these were God's people. They had their own opinion about things, which was not God's way.

Beloved, this shows that it's possible to be in the church and still be lost. 1 Peter 5:8 tells us we have an adversary who will do any and everything he can to destroy us. That is his purpose, to kill us.

> *Be sober, be vigilant; because your adversary the devil, as a roaring lion, walketh about, seeking whom he may devour.*

I don't care who you are; it is possible to get lost in the house (the church). From the man in the pulpit to the musician, choir member, deacon, or usher who mans the door, we all have been targeted. It is not enough just to come to church; we must *be* the church without spots, wrinkles, or blemishes.

It's sad to see people who have been in the church all their lives and who work in the church in many ways still go to hell. The Bible, the word of God, has clearly shown us the way. There is no other way—it's God's way only.

Remember what Elijah asked the people about their opinions (1 Kings 18:21)? Often we are led by our intellect and not by the spirit of God. Therefore, it becomes our way, our opinion, and not God's. In Proverbs 14:12, Solomon says,

> *There is a way which seemeth right unto a man, but the end thereof are the ways of death.*

Jesus reiterated this warning in Matthew 7:13-14,

> *Enter ye in at the strait gate: for wide is the gate, and broad is the way, that leadeth to destruction, and many there be which go in thereat: Because strait is the gate, and narrow is the way, which leadeth unto life, and few there be that find it.*

For the most part, the church people operate out of the flesh and not out of the spirit. The Bible calls this a carnal mind. There can be no accord, and it is not subject to the things of God.

> *For they that are after the flesh do mind the things of the flesh; but they that are after the Spirit the things of the Spirit. For to be carnally minded is death; but to be spiritually minded is life and peace. Because the carnal mind is enmity against God: for it is not subject to the law of God, neither indeed can be. So then they that are in the flesh cannot please God* (Romans 8:5-8).

I cry out to the church, let's not be lost in the house. Be obedient to Romans 12:1-2:

> *I beseech you therefore, brethren, by the mercies of God, that ye present your bodies a living sacrifice, holy, acceptable unto God, which is your reasonable service. And be not conformed to this world: but be ye transformed by the renewing of your mind, that ye may prove what is that good, and acceptable, and perfect, will of God.*

Renewal is essential for soundness in our thinking and actions. If we don't renew ourselves in the things of God, pretty soon our decisions will be based upon our own intellect and not the wisdom of God's word.

Many have become victimized by the cares of this life, this world. Jesus warned us about this in the parable of the sower.

> *Hear ye therefore the parable of the sower...He also that received seed among the thorns is he that heareth the word; and the care of this world, and the deceitfulness of riches, choke the word, and he becometh unfruitful* (Matthew 13:18, 22).

As of March 2018, I will be seventy-four years old. In all my years, I have not seen such a shift in faith as is taking place now. We are in a time when people are so selfish that the moral fabric of the country—and even of the church—has been lost to greed.

The house should be a place where people are saved, not a place they can be lost in. The attitude of the people has become so complacent, until the church has become reduced to just a social gathering without the power of demonstration by the Holy Ghost. This will all change once God reclaims His church.

Let me end this chapter with the parable of the ten virgins:

> *Then shall the kingdom of heaven be likened unto ten virgins, which took their lamps, and went forth to meet the bridegroom. And five of them were wise, and five were foolish. They that were foolish took their lamps, and took no oil with them: But the wise took oil in their vessels with their lamps. While the bridegroom tarried,*

they all slumbered and slept. And at midnight there was a cry made, Behold, the bridegroom cometh; go ye out to meet him. Then all those virgins arose, and trimmed their lamps. And the foolish said unto the wise, Give us of your oil; for our lamps are gone out. But the wise answered, saying, Not so; lest there be not enough for us and you: but go ye rather to them that sell, and buy for yourselves. And while they went to buy, the bridegroom came; and they that were ready went in with him to the marriage: and the door was shut. Afterward came also the other virgins, saying, Lord, Lord, open to us. But he answered and said, Verily I say unto you, I know you not. Watch therefore, for ye know neither the day nor the hour wherein the Son of man cometh (Matthew 25:1-13).

Don't be lost in the house!

God Is Taking Back His Church

CHAPTER THREE

The greed and selfishness that we are witnessing in our society is devastating, and the church is not exempt. For the most part, the leadership in our churches are humanistic, and the felonious acts of many church leaders are unconscionable. The narrative has changed. No longer is it by God's spirit; it is now about who has the biggest church and the most money.

We seem to think that the bigger the church, the more God's approval is upon it. It has become so bad that most televised church programs are fundraising and selling products.

Where is the gospel? Where is the preacher who preaches the Good News—the wages of sin, heaven, and hell—or prepares the people for the last days' work—the rapture of the church—or teaches about the need to be sanctified and live a holy lifestyle? None of this is the focus in today's churches. The Bible teaches that in the last days, our fight will not be against flesh and blood but against principalities and wickedness in all places of authority—and this includes our churches.

Finally, my brethren, be strong in the Lord, and in the power of his might. Put on the whole armour of God, that ye may be able to stand against the wiles of the devil. For we wrestle not against flesh and blood, but against principalities, against powers, against the rulers of the darkness of this world, against spiritual wickedness in high places. Wherefore take unto you the whole armour of God, that ye may be able to withstand in the evil day, and having done all, to stand (Ephesians 6:10-13).

Apostle Paul calls it an evil day, which we need to stand strong in the faith to overcome. Again, I reference Jude.

Jude, the servant of Jesus Christ, and brother of James, to them that are sanctified by God the Father, and preserved in Jesus Christ, and called: Mercy unto you, and peace, and love, be multiplied. Beloved, when I gave all diligence to write unto you of the common salvation, it was needful for me to write unto you, and exhort you that ye should earnestly contend for the faith which was once delivered unto the saints. For there are certain men crept in unawares, who were before of old ordained to this condemnation, ungodly men, turning the grace of our God into lasciviousness, and denying the only Lord God, and our Lord Jesus Christ.

I will therefore put you in remembrance, though ye once knew this, how that the Lord, having saved the people out of the land of Egypt, afterward destroyed them that believed not. And the angels which kept not their first estate, but left their own habitation, he hath reserved in everlasting chains under darkness unto the judgment of the great day. Even as Sodom and Gomorrha, and the cities about them in like manner, giving themselves over to fornication, and going after strange flesh, are set forth for an example, suffering the vengeance of eternal fire (Jude 1-7).

Let's face it, the church is in bad shape. Only a remnant is saved. Let me pause here and share a sermonic message that God gave me in May 2017, *The Coming Storm.*

• • •

The Coming Storm

SUNDAY, MAY 28, 2017

See that ye refuse not him that speaketh. For if they escaped not who refused him that spake on earth, much more shall not we escape, if we turn away from him that speaketh from heaven: Whose voice then shook the earth: but now he hath promised, saying, Yet once more I shake not the earth only, but also heaven. And this word, Yet once more, signifieth the removing of those things that are shaken, as of things that are made, that those things which cannot be shaken may remain. Wherefore we receiving a kingdom which cannot be moved, let us have grace, whereby we may serve God acceptably with reverence and godly fear: For our God is a consuming fire (Hebrews 12:25-29).

Behold, the Lord maketh the earth empty, and maketh it waste, and turneth it upside down, and scattereth abroad the inhabitants thereof. And it shall be, as with the people, so with the priest; as with the servant, so with his master; as with the maid, so with her mistress; as with the buyer, so with the seller; as with the lender, so with the borrower; as with the taker of usury, so with the giver of usury to him. The land shall be utterly emptied, and utterly spoiled: for the Lord hath spoken this word (Isaiah 24:1-3).

For some time now, I have preached about the coming storm that will shake things to its core. The storm will affect all areas of life, such as:

- Raises/hiring practices
- Health plans/investments/cost of living
- Racial tension increase
- Cuts in government-sponsored social programs:
    - Nursing homes
    - Section 8/daycares
    - Food stamps/Meals-on-Wheels

This will also result in the lifting of many governmental restrictions over big businesses consequently, big businesses will have the freedom to do what they will, both with their products and with their work force.

There will also be personal attacks on the world by demon spirits that will compromise or possess many individuals.

The only hope you will have is in the Lord. Many will be disappointed because most have religion and not a relationship, but merely having religion will not suffice.

With all that is going on in the earth, there must be preparation!

FOR THE CHURCH

God is taking His church back out of the hands of man and placing His church with pastors after His own heart.

Everything that is done without God will not stand and will fail.

I've preached about getting to a place in God where you can have stability and soundness of mind. The storm that is now upon us will be more than we can handle in our natural strength. We must stay connected to God and to the body. If we remain connected, we will never be overwhelmed.

Before the election, I shared with you who the Lord said was going to win. I also shared that the new administration would usher in a confusing and lying spirit, which would resonate throughout the whole administration. Many would be affected by this spirit, for it is the will of God that it be so.

There is a principle or law at work here: whatever is sown *shall be reaped!*

As a country, many have become very rich on the backs of the working class. Everywhere we look, we see selfish greedy leaders. One example is that of temporary workers. A temp agency is an organization with a plan to keep a person working while half of their pay goes to the agency.

We must understand that most people who are in authority do not care about their subjects, so God has sent a spirit of confusion to frustrate our leaders and bring about division to work His plan.

We all know that a house divided against itself cannot stand.

HISTORY

This is not the first time God sent a lying and confusing spirit to disrupt the people. 1 Kings 22:19-23 tells the story of King Ahab. The king was upset with the prophet Micaiah and had him imprisoned, where he was fed bread and water.

> *And he said, Hear thou therefore the word of the Lord: I saw the Lord sitting on his throne, and all the host of heaven standing by him on his right hand and on his left. And the Lord said, Who shall persuade Ahab, that he may go up and fall at Ramothgilead? And one said on this manner, and another said on that manner. And there came forth a spirit, and stood before the Lord, and said, I will persuade him. And the Lord said unto him, Wherewith? And he said, I will go forth, and I will be a lying spirit in the mouth of all his prophets. And he said, Thou shalt persuade him, and prevail also: go forth, and do so. Now therefore, behold, the Lord hath put a lying spirit in the mouth of all these thy prophets, and the Lord hath spoken evil concerning thee* (1 Kings 22:19-23).

As you can see from this passage, the disruption and confusion was not about the devil, but rather about what God was doing. Despite the confusion, people want to hear good things spoken over America. By its very nature, power without God corrupts people and that's in every arena.

The storm is upon us because of the ungodly acts of our leaders and nation. We all have a choice: we can be blessed in it or destroyed by it. Unfortunately, fasting and prayer will not stop what's coming. This is America's harvest, her just dues.

Church, our adversaries are many and all around us, so it will be beyond our ability to help. It's every man for himself. This is the time when everyone must be established in their own faith. For this to happen, God must take back His church and establish her in righteousness. To all of you who are established in the Lord, He is saying,

> *Be not dismayed or afraid because of this storm. Though it be great, you will win and not suffer loss, because the battle is not yours, it's Mine.*
>
> *You will not have to fight in the battle; just stand still and see the salvation of the Lord. Watch me work!*

Just like in 2 Chronicles, it was spoken to King Jehoshaphat and the people that they would not have to fight; instead they had to

- believe in the Lord—So you shall be established;
- believe His prophets—So you shall prosper;
- appoint singers unto the Lord; and
- praise the Lord for the beauty of holiness.

Holiness was the cry word. It is not preached in today's churches. And as the people went singing, they praised the Lord, for His mercy endures forever. When they began to praise the Lord, God set traps against the enemy.

Let me end with this:

> *The Lord is my light and my salvation; whom shall I fear? the Lord is the strength of my life; of whom shall I be afraid? When the wicked, even mine enemies and my foes, came upon me to eat up my flesh, they stumbled and fell. Though an host should encamp against me, my*

heart shall not fear: though war should rise against me, in this will I be confident. One thing have I desired of the Lord, that will I seek after; that I may dwell in the house of the Lord all the days of my life, to behold the beauty of the Lord, and to enquire in his temple. For in the time of trouble he shall hide me in his pavilion: in the secret of his tabernacle shall he hide me; he shall set me up upon a rock. And now shall mine head be lifted up above mine enemies round about me: therefore will I offer in his tabernacle sacrifices of joy; I will sing, yea, I will sing praises unto the Lord...I had fainted, unless I had believed to see the goodness of the Lord in the land of the living. Wait on the Lord: be of good courage, and he shall strengthen thine heart: wait, I say, on the Lord (Psalm 27:1-6, 13-14).

Tell somebody, "It's the Lord's battle!"

• • •

The Lord is reclaiming His church, and when it is over, He will have a kingdom (a people) that cannot be moved. Get ready, for the time is now. Many will be on the outside looking in and wondering what happened to their ministry. It's simple: it wasn't of God and so God shut it down.

We can see how many have placed their name on the work, taking ownership of it instead of God. The glory is theirs and not the Lord's. Shame on them.

This type of self-gratification is a thing of the past as God completes the takeover. What a great day! I am looking forward to it. Under the headship of Christ, the whole body will once again become sound. To the called, God is on the move to reestablish His church in righteousness.

To the called, we are it. It's our time. Our prayer is this:

Lord, here we are humbly submitting ourselves to Your will. Take us and make us the vessel that we ought to be. Cause our hearts to be restored in Your love that we might walk in love's mission, giving our ourselves so that others can be saved. Amen.

Time Travelers

CHAPTER FOUR

Understanding Time and Satan's Use of It

Time, by its very nature, is transitory, and therefore, it is always moving. It has its seasons and cycles. It has a starting point and a finishing point. The whole world and all of creation are set in time. The question is, therefore, when did time begin? In this chapter, you will know how much time plays a part in our lives.

Time began when creation was introduced to death and decay, and it all started with the fall of Adam and Eve. In creation, there was no death, only life. Let's read Genesis 1:26-31.

> *And God said, Let us make man in our image, after our likeness: and let them have dominion over the fish of the sea, and over the fowl of the air, and over the cattle, and over all the earth, and over every creeping thing that creepeth upon the earth. So God created man in his own image, in the image of God created he him; male and female created he them. And God blessed them, and God*

said unto them, Be fruitful, and multiply, and replenish the earth, and subdue it: and have dominion over the fish of the sea, and over the fowl of the air, and over every living thing that moveth upon the earth. And God said, Behold, I have given you every herb bearing seed, which is upon the face of all the earth, and every tree, in the which is the fruit of a tree yielding seed; to you it shall be for meat. And to every beast of the earth, and to every fowl of the air, and to every thing that creepeth upon the earth, wherein there is life, I have given every green herb for meat: and it was so. And God saw every thing that he had made, and, behold, it was very good. And the evening and the morning were the sixth day.

Death was introduced in Genesis 2:15-17:

And the Lord God took the man, and put him into the garden of Eden to dress it and to keep it. And the Lord God commanded the man, saying, Of every tree of the garden thou mayest freely eat: But of the tree of the knowledge of good and evil, thou shalt not eat of it: for in the day that thou eatest thereof thou shalt surely die.

When Adam and Eve ate of the forbidden fruit, right then, mankind was placed in time, along with all of creation that they had dominion over. Once placed in time, everything started to die because sin had cursed it.

First the seasons, Ecclesiastes 3:1-8.

To every thing there is a season, and a time to every purpose under the heaven:

A time to be born, and a time to die; a time to plant, and a time to pluck up that which is planted;

> *A time to kill, and a time to heal; a time to break down, and a time to build up;*
>
> *A time to weep, and a time to laugh; a time to mourn, and a time to dance;*
>
> *A time to cast away stones, and a time to gather stones together; a time to embrace, and a time to refrain from embracing;*
>
> *A time to get, and a time to lose; a time to keep, and a time to cast away;*
>
> *A time to rend, and a time to sew; a time to keep silence, and a time to speak;*
>
> *A time to love, and a time to hate; a time of war, and a time of peace.*

We see that everything started out to be everlasting until sin entered the world. Once sin entered, everything started to die. God already had a plan to restore His creation. That was His nature.

The bad part about time, apart from death, was that everything in it was vanity, as King Solomon found and wrote in Ecclesiastes 2:1-11:

> *I said in mine heart, Go to now, I will prove thee with mirth, therefore enjoy pleasure: and, behold, this also is vanity.*
>
> *I said of laughter, It is mad: and of mirth, What doeth it?*
>
> *I sought in mine heart to give myself unto wine, yet acquainting mine heart with wisdom; and to lay hold on folly, till I might see what was that good for the sons of men, which they should do under the heaven all the days of their life.*

I made me great works; I builded me houses; I planted me vineyards:

I made me gardens and orchards, and I planted trees in them of all kind of fruits:

I made me pools of water, to water therewith the wood that bringeth forth trees:

I got me servants and maidens, and had servants born in my house; also I had great possessions of great and small cattle above all that were in Jerusalem before me:

I gathered me also silver and gold, and the peculiar treasure of kings and of the provinces: I gat me men singers and women singers, and the delights of the sons of men, as musical instruments, and that of all sorts.

So I was great, and increased more than all that were before me in Jerusalem: also my wisdom remained with me.

And whatsoever mine eyes desired I kept not from them, I withheld not my heart from any joy; for my heart rejoiced in all my labour: and this was my portion of all my labour.

Then I looked on all the works that my hands had wrought, and on the labour that I had laboured to do: and, behold, all was vanity and vexation of spirit, and there was no profit under the sun.

In creation, all things were good and working together for the good of man. After the fall, all things were working against him for his destruction because the dominion of the earth was lost to Satan. In spite of this, God created a way that we (creation) would be saved and that was through His redemptive work on the cross. Then He gave us His written word, to survive time.

I remember several years ago, in 2011, I lost one of my sisters, May, at the beginning of the year, and by the end of that same year, I lost another sister, Jessie. That was a hard time in my life. I was called upon to do the eulogy. I will never forget the word God gave me—*Surviving Time.*

I remember saying that time was all about dying. Satan was given dominion over all that is of the earth, even our earthly bodies that we call flesh. Because of the enmity between him and God, Satan's plan is to wreck the whole world and destroy mankind, which was created in God's image. He's like that, you know. He loves to destroy because he is still mad about being kicked out of heaven.

Now we can understand that time is a killer and that we can only get through it in Christ by walking and living in the spirit. The Bible tells us that flesh and blood shall not inherit the kingdom of God.

The world has been designed by Satan to cause us to live in the flesh, knowing that if this happens, we cannot be saved.

> *There is therefore now no condemnation to them which are in Christ Jesus, who walk not after the flesh, but after the Spirit. For the law of the Spirit of life in Christ Jesus hath made me free from the law of sin and death. For what the law could not do, in that it was weak through the flesh, God sending his own Son in the likeness of sinful flesh, and for sin, condemned sin in the flesh: That the righteousness of the law might be fulfilled in us, who walk not after the flesh, but after the Spirit. For they that are after the flesh do mind the things of the flesh; but they that are after the Spirit the things of the Spirit.*
>
> *For to be carnally minded is death; but to be spiritually minded is life and peace. Because the carnal*

> *mind is enmity against God: for it is not subject to the law of God, neither indeed can be. So then they that are in the flesh cannot please God. But ye are not in the flesh, but in the Spirit, if so be that the Spirit of God dwell in you. Now if any man have not the Spirit of Christ, he is none of his. And if Christ be in you, the body is dead because of sin; but the Spirit is life because of righteousness. But if the Spirit of him that raised up Jesus from the dead dwell in you, he that raised up Christ from the dead shall also quicken your mortal bodies by his Spirit that dwelleth in you. Therefore, brethren, we are debtors, not to the flesh, to live after the flesh* (Romans 8:1-12).

I am asking you to digest that for a little while.

Everyone has been appointed a season in time. They have a purpose in time, and there is an expiration date. Everyone's season is different in length, but they will have enough time to finish their purpose or course of work. The only way we can survive time is to stay the course, and by doing so, all things will work for our good. If we do not stay the course, all things will work for our death.

> *And we know that all things work together for good to them that love God, to them who are the called according to his purpose. For whom he did foreknow, he also did predestinate to be conformed to the image of his Son, that he might be the firstborn among many brethren. Moreover whom he did predestinate, them he also called: and whom he called, them he also justified: and whom he justified, them he also glorified. What shall we then say to these things? If God be for us, who can be against us?*

> *He that spared not his own Son, but delivered him up for us all, how shall he not with him also freely give us all things?* (Romans 8:28-32).

We see here that the apostle Paul is asking us a question about the possibility of separation.

> *Who shall separate us from the love of Christ? shall tribulation, or distress, or persecution, or famine, or nakedness, or peril, or sword? As it is written, For thy sake we are killed all the day long; we are accounted as sheep for the slaughter. Nay, in all these things we are more than conquerors through him that loved us. For I am persuaded, that neither death, nor life, nor angels, nor principalities, nor powers, nor things present, nor things to come, Nor height, nor depth, nor any other creature, shall be able to separate us from the love of God, which is in Christ Jesus our Lord* (Romans 8:35-39).

As you can see, it is possible to survive time, if we are wise. In time, wisdom is so important.

> *Hear, ye children, the instruction of a father, and attend to know understanding.*
>
> *For I give you good doctrine, forsake ye not my law.*
>
> *For I was my father's son, tender and only beloved in the sight of my mother.*
>
> *He taught me also, and said unto me, Let thine heart retain my words: keep my commandments, and live.*
>
> *Get wisdom, get understanding: forget it not; neither decline from the words of my mouth.*
>
> *Forsake her not, and she shall preserve thee: love her, and she shall keep thee.*

Wisdom is the principal thing; therefore get wisdom: and with all thy getting get understanding.

Exalt her, and she shall promote thee: she shall bring thee to honour, when thou dost embrace her (Proverbs 4:1-8).

Life is a one-time deal. There are no do-overs or resets. The decisions we make will bless or curse us in this life. They will lead us to eternal life or eternal death. This is based upon how we choose, and therefore, we need to make wise decisions.

So then, what is wisdom? It is the ability to use or apply knowledge wisely. Knowledge is having information or the condition of being informed. It is our job to inform the lost.

One of the main reasons for not surviving time is procrastination. We all must work hard to overcome its grip. It is time to get up and get back in the race of time. We must finish our course.

Have you ever thought about what happened to people who died suddenly? Did they finish their course? Tomorrow is not promised; remember, time is preparing us for eternity. If we do the time just right, we will never die. When my time has ended, I am expecting to hear, "Well done, My good and faithful servant!"

To the called, remember all that is of the world that Satan can use is

- the lust of the eye,
- the lust of the flesh, and
- the pride of life.

My hope is that this chapter has taught us the danger of time if not used wisely.

Let me leave you with this thought. Even though we are placed in time, we can be citizens of the eternal. Remember, we are pilgrims and strangers in the earth, and this is not our home. We are time travelers, so don't get caught up in the time and forget you are on a mission and just pass through.

Transformation

CHAPTER FIVE

One of the things that is expected of us during our travel through time is transformation. Transformation is a time to get the image restored. When Adam fell, the image of God was lost. As the sin nature of everyone born to Adam was passed on, all of mankind was born into sin and shaped in iniquity, and by our very sin nature, we all were hell bound. For we know that flesh and blood cannot enter the kingdom of God.

In time, we have been given the opportunity to choose. We must understand that when we choose the kingdom of God, we must expect change and change never comes easy. Can you remember a time when you or some acquaintance of yours tried to break a habit? Was it easy? The response is always, no. So transformation won't come easy.

The problem is that the church has been in a state of decline for so long that we think who we are is who we are supposed to be. According to God's word, we are well below the targeted mark that God has set for us. Before we can hope for change, we must accept the fact that we need change.

But change is not just for the sake of changing. In changing, we will complete the process of becoming the full measure and stature of Jesus Christ. The Bible tells us that it does not yet appear what we shall be, but that we shall be like Him.

We must become more like Jesus in order to finish our course. We must be like Him

- in our character, integrity, and faithfulness;
- by demonstrating love, righteousness, and holiness;
- by knowing the things of God;
- by relying on the Holy Ghost power of demonstration; and
- by revealing God's kingdom.

According to Apostle Paul, there must be a demonstration of power:

> *And I, brethren, when I came to you, came not with excellency of speech or of wisdom, declaring unto you the testimony of God. For I determined not to know any thing among you, save Jesus Christ, and him crucified. And I was with you in weakness, and in fear, and in much trembling. And my speech and my preaching was not with enticing words of man's wisdom, but in demonstration of the Spirit and of power: That your faith should not stand in the wisdom of men, but in the power of God* (1 Corinthians 2:1-5).

We must understand that we have become a part of the church in a season when most of the church has been lost. Are we not the sons of God and joint heirs with Christ?

For ye have not received the spirit of bondage again to fear; but ye have received the Spirit of adoption, whereby we cry, Abba, Father. The Spirit itself beareth witness with our spirit, that we are the children of God: And if children, then heirs; heirs of God, and joint-heirs with Christ; if so be that we suffer with him, that we may be also glorified together (Romans 8:15-17).

Transformation begins when receiving the word of God. When it sprouts, it is a seed. It is planted in our hearts, and that gives us a new mindset. If the mind is not changed, then nothing has changed. Let's read Romans 12:1-3:

I beseech you therefore, brethren, by the mercies of God, that ye present your bodies a living sacrifice, holy, acceptable unto God, which is your reasonable service. And be not conformed to this world: but be ye transformed by the renewing of your mind, that ye may prove what is that good, and acceptable, and perfect, will of God. For I say, through the grace given unto me, to every man that is among you, not to think of himself more highly than he ought to think; but to think soberly, according as God hath dealt to every man the measure of faith.

Once transformation (the change) takes place, it gives us access to the mind of God so we will know and do the will of God.

But as it is written, Eye hath not seen, nor ear heard, neither have entered into the heart of man, the things which God hath prepared for them that love him. But God hath revealed them unto us by his Spirit: for the Spirit searcheth all things, yea, the deep things of God. For what man knoweth the things of a man, save the

> *spirit of man which is in him? even so the things of God knoweth no man, but the Spirit of God. Now we have received, not the spirit of the world, but the spirit which is of God; that we might know the things that are freely given to us of God* (1 Corinthians 2:9-12).

> *For who hath known the mind of the Lord, that he may instruct him? but we have the mind of Christ* (1 Corinthians 2:16).

I would like to conclude with a sermon I presented on transformation in 2015. We must remember that a season with God is not a four-month period or a four-year period. God sets the seasons and makes them long enough to complete His work.

• • •

The Time of Transformation—Harvest

SEPTEMBER 2015

> *Behold, what manner of love the Father hath bestowed upon us, that we should be called the sons of God: therefore the world knoweth us not, because it knew him not. Beloved, now are we the sons of God, and it doth not yet appear what we shall be: but we know that, when he shall appear, we shall be like him; for we shall see him as he is. And every man that hath this hope in him purifieth himself, even as he is pure* (1 John 3:1-3).

When this statement was made, the church, the sons of God, had not fully been *transformed*. John explained that what was now being seen was not how the church will be.

This statement was made over 2,000 years ago. *Not yet* was then, but this is now.

The time or season of transformation is at hand. It's time to be like Jesus; for salvation purposes, Christ must be revealed.

In Romans 8:19, Paul states that all creation is waiting on us to be revealed. This cannot take place until the transformation is complete.

Let's face it; as of now, we, the church, are not walking in the anointing that the early church had. The Bible teaches that a restoration is coming, and when it comes, the later church and works will be greater than the former.

So the question is, how long will God wait before the transformation process begins? He has placed things in seasons. The word *season* in short means the time of or for something. Season is a principle or a time that God has set in place. Generally, whatever is to happen happens within its season.

Look what the preacher says in Ecclesiastes 3:1:

> *To every thing there is a season, which is a time to fulfill purpose; the power of a season is in the season.*

Why do I feel this is the season of transformation?

- It has been revealed to me in the spirit.
- It correlates with the last of the four blood moons and the time of feast of the tabernacle.
- It's the year of jubilee on the Jewish calendar.

I did not know all this when God gave me this year's focus.

If the *transformation* is not complete in us during its season, it probably will not happen. It is very unlikely that a thing produces out of season.

What are some of the signs that we are in the season of transformation?

- fires
- floods
- extreme weather—cold/snow/heat
- the economy
- society—racial violence/same-sex marriage
- the increase of knowledge (e.g., cell phones)

The cell phone has increased knowledge greatly and made it easily accessible. Any signal that is in the air or information that is on the web is accessible to you by way of the cell phone.

Church, I believe the time is now. Last year, He told us the things that He was going to do in the earth: restore His name and take away the reproach from His church. This season is about Christ and His church.

> *Beloved, now are we the sons of God, and it does not yet appear what we shall be but we know that, when he shall appear, we shall be like him; for we shall see him as he is* (1 John 3:2).

So what does it mean to be like Him or to be transformed? It means to walk in His

- anointing,
- nature,
- calling, and
- power.

So when you see us, the church, you see Christ. Rise up…oh sleeping church.

With all the things that are going on in our society, if for no other reason, there needs to be a revealing of the true church for balance purposes. God will not stand back and let darkness take over; He said wherever sin abounds, much more grace abounds. So we must be fully *transformed* in order to release God's grace through the power of the Holy Ghost with demonstration.

For too long, the church has been inconsistent in who we are. It's time to overcome the influence of our flesh.

Life is in the seed. The life of the seed is released when it is placed in the right conditions, and it grows inside until it busts out. The word is God's seed, and *we are simply the soil for the seed.*

The good news is that it will be God who gives the increase. He alone will receive the glory! When the transformation is completed, there will be no more back and forth struggle with our flesh. We will be like Him, period! Revival will also come with the transformation. Our responsibility is simply to be in the right place.

What is the right place? The right place is

- a place of love,
- a place of peace (no fighting among each other),
- a place of faith,
- a place of righteousness,
- a place of expectancy, and
- a place of surrendering to His will.

Jesus told His church to come out of the world and be separated and not touch the unclean things. Only then would He be our God and we His people. Only then would He walk in us and talk through us.

We are His chosen ones, to reveal His kingdom.

The time has come, so let the transformation begin. He is here to complete us, for we are complete in Him.

So I beseech you brethren, by the mercies of God, that you present your bodies a living sacrifice, holy and acceptable unto God; this is your reasonable service. And do not think like this world, but be *transformed* by the renewing of your mind and prove what is the good, acceptable, and perfect *will of God.* There it is, *a new mindset*. For as a person thinks, so is he.

• • •

In my studies, I came across the following information that I will include here, from *The Fall Feast* by Dan Goodwin.

(The dates included are from 2015.)

- The Feast of the Trumpets was set for September 14, 2015. It is a type of the rapture of the church.
- The Day of Atonement (Hebrew, *Yom-Hakkippurim*) is a time of purification that must be completed before the next feast.
- The Feast of Booths or Tabernacles is a feast of transition from the Israelites' journey to entering the Promised Land, their destination.

On September 13, 2015 the eve of the Feast of Trumpets, there would be a solar eclipse.

September 23, 2015 is the beginning of the Feast of Atonement. Once every forty-nine years it culminates with the Year of Jubilee, and 2015 was that year, according to theologians. It is a time when all things are restored.

Sound the trumpet, for Jubilee is the last feast.

September 28 is the Feast of Tabernacles, when the last or fourth blood moon will be visible to Jerusalem.

This is our season of *transition, restoration* and *transformation.* It's time to bust out of the flesh and become like Jesus. *It is time to be set free! Stand up and be changed!*

Fire Makes Us Better

CHAPTER SIX

In order for a transformation to be fully completed, there must be the test of fire. We must understand that nothing is released for public consumption or use until it has been proven.

The 16th chapter of Exodus tells of a time when God was preparing the people to enter the Promised Land, but before He would let them in, they had to be proven. In this chapter, He rained down bread from heaven to prove the people. He instructed them to take just enough for one day at a time. Some of the people could not trust God's word that the next day He would rain down bread again. Those who couldn't trust God's word gathered much more than needed, but none of what they gathered lasted until the morning.

In this test, God was testing to see if they trusted His word. I am sure we all have been tested many times. In this chapter, I want us to look at how fire makes us better.

> *Blessed be the God and Father of our Lord Jesus Christ, which according to his abundant mercy hath begotten us again unto a lively hope by the resurrection of Jesus Christ from the dead, To an inheritance incorruptible, and*

undefiled, and that fadeth not away, reserved in heaven for you, Who are kept by the power of God through faith unto salvation ready to be revealed in the last time. Wherein ye greatly rejoice, though now for a season, if need be, ye are in heaviness through manifold temptations: That the trial of your faith, being much more precious than of gold that perisheth, though it be tried with fire, might be found unto praise and honour and glory at the appearing of Jesus Christ (1 Peter 1:3-7).

The hour of desperation is upon us. The scripture calls it a time of perplexing, vexation, and stress of nations. During this season, any kind of unity is at a premium. You will find it hard to find people getting along. Family members are being alienated, and our government is fragmented. It is impossible for there to be any lasting unity without Christ in the mix. Isolation will destroy many. As soon as people are offended, in most cases, they alienate themselves. Ask yourself, do I have a companion when I am going through fire or do I isolate myself?

When we isolate ourselves, we become a target. The minute we become detached, we are weakened. Satan's plan is to divide and conquer. The root problem is twofold. First, many don't know the value of family unity. Second, many are easily offended and without the ability to recognize that the fight is not against flesh and blood but spirits.

Offense Comes

Offense can only happen when people are in the flesh. The sad part is, they don't know that they are in the flesh, and without knowing it, they become victimized emotionally. How is it that people are so easily provoked emotionally?

It's a systematic problem that goes back to the time of transformation. No system is in place to help with the transformation process, so a lot of our flesh remains a part of us. For us to be emotionally hurt, we must first believe that we have been victimized. How can that be if God is in control of our life? With a sound mindset, which Christ gave us, we cannot be hurt emotionally. We must know that God has laid out a plan for our lives, the things that we encounter, and even the fire trial. It all works for our good.

Until we mature emotionally, we will never reach our destiny. We let people and things hold us back. The apostle Paul described it as being the *mark*, the high calling of God. When we reach that place in God, then nothing hurts us. Then we can truly say, it's all God, even the fire.

The fire makes us better! If you know this, then do as the apostle James did and count it all joy! It's hard to reach the overcomer's status. To get there, fire is required. Overcoming is not about people and things. It is and always will be about the soundness of our minds and having the ability to renew our minds. Because in the end, it all winds up in the mind. People, worries, fears, unbelief, and hopelessness—this is what we must overcome. We can't begin to live until we are overcomers.

Revelation 21:1-4, 8, 7—read in this order:

> *And I saw a new heaven and a new earth: for the first heaven and the first earth were passed away; and there was no more sea. And I John saw the holy city, new Jerusalem, coming down from God out of heaven, prepared as a bride adorned for her husband. And I heard a great voice out of heaven saying, Behold, the tabernacle*

of God is with men, and he will dwell with them, and they shall be his people, and God himself shall be with them, and be their God. And God shall wipe away all tears from their eyes; and there shall be no more death, neither sorrow, nor crying, neither shall there be any more pain: for the former things are passed away.

But the fearful, and unbelieving, and the abominable, and murderers, and whoremongers, and sorcerers, and idolaters, and all liars, shall have their part in the lake which burneth with fire and brimstone: which is the second death.

He that overcometh shall inherit all things; and I will be his God, and he shall be my son.

My brethren, count it all joy when ye fall into divers temptations; Knowing this, that the trying of your faith worketh patience. But let patience have her perfect work, that ye may be perfect and entire, wanting nothing (James 1:2-4).

Blessed be the God and Father of our Lord Jesus Christ, which according to his abundant mercy hath begotten us again unto a lively hope by the resurrection of Jesus Christ from the dead, To an inheritance incorruptible, and undefiled, and that fadeth not away, reserved in heaven for you, Who are kept by the power of God through faith unto salvation ready to be revealed in the last time. Wherein ye greatly rejoice, though now for a season, if need be, ye are in heaviness through manifold temptations: That the trial of your faith, being much more precious than of gold that perisheth, though it be tried with fire, might be found unto praise and honour and glory at the appearing of Jesus Christ (1 Peter 1:3-7).

Place your head between your hands and say, "Mind I renew you. You are restored, and you will not be in bondage any longer to worries, fears, sorrow, or hopelessness that leads to unbelief."

> *For the weapons of our warfare are not carnal, but mighty through God to the pulling down of strong holds; Casting down imaginations, and every high thing that exalteth itself against the knowledge of God, and bringing into captivity every thought to the obedience of Christ* (2 Corinthians 10:4-5).

You will not be troubled. I speak peace to you, and you will be obedient to the word of God. Amen.

Find someone and tell them, "The fire makes us better, for we glory in tribulations, tribulations work patience, patience gives us experience, and experience gives us hope!"

Back to the Future: A Time of Purification

CHAPTER SEVEN

In chapter six, the focus was on the fire and how it makes us better. I am sure that we all know that fire can destroy or cleanse. Fire also has the ability to purify. As you know by now, God does everything for a purpose. Fire is getting us ready for the work.

There is a mighty move of God that is coming in the near future. This move will involve His church—not all, but only those who are ready. It's back to the future.

God has been pleading with His church for some time now to recommit to the things of His kingdom. A few years ago, God gave me a message concerning *sanctifying His name on earth* by the repairing of the breach. In 2016, the focus was on *transformation in preparation for the last day's work.* Church, we are being led somewhere, a place that we, this generation, has never been before.

It is like it was with Moses; God called him and the people back to the future and let them know that their future was found in the past, the place that he had given to Abraham. This inheritance was lost over time because of sin.

Let's visit their journey. As we pick up in Joshua 1, God had them en route back to the place of the call of

Abraham, their father. By now, Moses was dead and the responsibility of leadership fell on Joshua. Let's read:

> *Now after the death of Moses the servant of the Lord it came to pass, that the Lord spake unto Joshua the son of Nun, Moses' minister, saying, Moses my servant is dead; now therefore arise, go over this Jordan, thou, and all this people, unto the land which I do give to them, even to the children of Israel. Every place that the sole of your foot shall tread upon, that have I given unto you, as I said unto Moses. From the wilderness and this Lebanon even unto the great river, the river Euphrates, all the land of the Hittites, and unto the great sea toward the going down of the sun, shall be your coast.*
>
> *There shall not any man be able to stand before thee all the days of thy life: as I was with Moses, so I will be with thee: I will not fail thee, nor forsake thee. Be strong and of a good courage: for unto this people shalt thou divide for an inheritance the land, which I sware unto their fathers to give them. Only be thou strong and very courageous, that thou mayest observe to do according to all the law, which Moses my servant commanded thee: turn not from it to the right hand or to the left, that thou mayest prosper withersoever thou goest. This book of the law shall not depart out of thy mouth; but thou shalt meditate therein day and night, that thou mayest observe to do according to all that is written therein: for then thou shalt make thy way prosperous, and then thou shalt have good success. Have not I commanded thee? Be strong and of a good courage; be not afraid, neither be thou dismayed: for the Lord thy God is with thee whithersoever thou goest* (Joshua 1:1-9).

If you look closely, you can see this was what God was doing. All He needed the people to do was to follow His lead.

In chapter three, the people were making plans to cross the Jordan River into their future, which was their past.

> *And Joshua rose early in the morning; and they removed from Shittim, and came to Jordan, he and all the children of Israel, and lodged there before they passed over. And it came to pass after three days, that the officers went through the host; And they commanded the people, saying, When ye see the ark of the covenant of the Lord your God, and the priests the Levites bearing it, then ye shall remove from your place, and go after it. Yet there shall be a space between you and it, about two thousand cubits by measure: come not near unto it, that ye may know the way by which ye must go: for ye have not passed this way heretofore. And Joshua said unto the people, Sanctify yourselves: for to morrow the Lord will do wonders among you. And Joshua spake unto the priests, saying, Take up the ark of the covenant, and pass over before the people. And they took up the ark of the covenant, and went before the people. And the Lord said unto Joshua, This day will I begin to magnify thee in the sight of all Israel, that they may know that, as I was with Moses, so I will be with thee (Joshua 3:1-7).*

As you can see, before God would bring them into their future, they first had to be sanctified, for this was the place of milk and honey, a holy place. Today we find ourselves in the move of God being brought back to the place of origin. This is the place where the disciples trod.

Here is what the Bible says about that place:

> *Even when we were dead in sins, hath quickened us together with Christ, (by grace ye are saved;) And hath raised us up together, and made us sit together in heavenly places in Christ Jesus: That in the ages to come he might shew the exceeding riches of his grace in his kindness toward us through Christ Jesus. For by grace are ye saved through faith; and that not of yourselves: it is the gift of God: Not of works, lest any man should boast. For we are his workmanship, created in Christ Jesus unto good works, which God hath before ordained that we should walk in them (Ephesians 2:5-10).*

About that place He says:

- Behold, I give you the keys to the kingdom.
- If you abide in Me and My word in you, you can ask what you will, and it shall be done.
- I give you power over all the power of your enemy.
- No weapon formed against you shall prosper.
- Houses that you did not build I will give to you.
- All things will work for your good.

As He was with Paul and Silas, James and John, Peter and the others, so is He with us. He will not leave us nor forsake us. He will not fail us, for He always remains the same. It is His will that we, the church, reclaim our inheritance, the anointing that Jude talked about. Before we can get settled in our inheritance, we must first prove our faith.

We are fighting the world, the flesh, and Satan. The fight should not be this hard, and we should be enjoying the milk and honey. It's time to cross over to the place of milk and honey and the place of rest. For there *still* remains *a place of rest* for the people of God. It is moving day, and we are going to a better place, so we must get rid of some stuff. It's back to the future for us!

> *And Joshua said unto the people, Sanctify yourselves: for tomorrow the Lord will do wonders among you* (Joshua 3:5).

To the called, God is waiting on us, so let's get moving!

Revealing the Glory

CHAPTER EIGHT

Revealing God's glory is so important for the end-time movement, and we must position ourselves to do so.

> *For I reckon that the sufferings of this present time are not worthy to be compared with the glory which shall be revealed in us. For the earnest expectation of the creature waiteth for the manifestation of the sons of God* (Romans 8:18-19).

We see that all the suffering was to prepare us for this time, the glory time. The glory that I speak of is the supernatural manifestation (of some kind) of the kingdom of God into the physical realm. Remember what Thomas said? "Unless I see the nail prints in His hands and thrust my finger into his side, I will not believe He has risen."

The Season of the Tabernacle Glory

To understand the glory of God, we must look at the history of the glory being revealed in the Old Testament.

And Moses and Aaron and his sons washed their hands and their feet thereat: When they went into the tent of the congregation, and when they came near unto the altar, they washed; as the Lord commanded Moses. And he reared up the court round about the tabernacle and the altar, and set up the hanging of the court gate. So Moses finished the work. Then a cloud covered the tent of the congregation, and the glory of the Lord filled the tabernacle. And Moses was not able to enter into the tent of the congregation, because the cloud abode thereon, and the glory of the Lord filled the tabernacle. And when the cloud was taken up from over the tabernacle, the children of Israel went onward in all their journeys: But if the cloud were not taken up, then they journeyed not till the day that it was taken up. For the cloud of the Lord was upon the tabernacle by day, and fire was on it by night, in the sight of all the house of Israel, throughout all their journeys (Exodus 40:31-38).

The glory of God manifested itself in the *tabernacle* during the wilderness dwelling. The tabernacle was a tent in the wilderness.

The Season of the Temple Glory

The glory of God then manifested itself in the *temple,* during the Promised Land dwelling

Thus all the work that Solomon made for the house of the Lord was finished: and Solomon brought in all the things that David his father had dedicated; and the silver, and the gold, and all the instruments, put he

among the treasures of the house of God. It came even to pass, as the trumpeters and singers were as one, to make one sound to be heard in praising and thanking the Lord; and when they lifted up their voice with the trumpets and cymbals and instruments of musick, and praised the Lord, saying, For he is good; for his mercy endureth for ever: that then the house was filled with a cloud, even the house of the Lord; So that the priests could not stand to minister by reason of the cloud: for the glory of the Lord had filled the house of God (2 Chronicles 5:1, 13, 14).

As you can see, once again God's glory showed up. This began another transition, which we will see as we move towards the New Testament and the new covenant.

There was a change of the priesthood from the tribe of the Levites to Judah. The tribe of the Levites were the descendants of the third son of Jacob, Levi. His name, Levi, means a joining. All other tribes had a portion of land as their inheritance, but not the Levites; they were a tribe of priests. They were keepers and servers of the temple. They were God's helpers. God was their portion.

The Transition to the New Testament

- New tribe: Judah—praise
- New order of priesthood and chief priest
- The new chief priest was of the order of Melchizedek
- A new covenant
- A new dwelling place—temple

In all the Old Testament dwelling places of God, when they were open for business, the glory of God showed up. Now we are in the New Testament age with the new temple. We the church are the temple of God in these last days. Jesus said, *"I will build My church, the dwelling place, and the gates of hell shall not prevail against it."*

The New Testament Church

On opening day:

> *And when the day of Pentecost was fully come, they were all with one accord in one place. And suddenly there came a sound from heaven as of a rushing mighty wind, and it filled all the house where they were sitting. And there appeared unto them cloven tongues like as of fire, and it sat upon each of them. And they were all filled with the Holy Ghost, and began to speak with other tongues, as the Spirit gave them utterance. Others mocking said, These men are full of new wine. But Peter, standing up with the eleven, lifted up his voice, and said unto them, Ye men of Judaea, and all ye that dwell at Jerusalem, be this known unto you, and hearken to my words: For these are not drunken, as ye suppose, seeing it is but the third hour of the day.*
>
> *But this is that which was spoken by the prophet Joel; And it shall come to pass in the last days, saith God, I will pour out of my Spirit upon all flesh: and your sons and your daughters shall prophesy, and your young men shall see visions, and your old men shall dream dreams: And on my servants and on my handmaidens I will pour out in those days of my Spirit; and*

> *they shall prophesy: And I will shew wonders in heaven above, and signs in the earth beneath; blood, and fire, and vapour of smoke: The sun shall be turned into darkness, and the moon into blood, before the great and notable day of the Lord come: And it shall come to pass, that whosoever shall call on the name of the Lord shall be saved* (Acts 2:1-4, 13-21).

Once again, as God's dwelling place was open for business, His glory showed up. In this one day, about 3,000 souls were added to the church. The point is, whenever God begins to move, His glory first invades His temple. The temple is His dwelling place, and He operates out of His dwelling place.

A Time of Restoration

In the Old Testament, there were times when the temple was destroyed and only the foundation remained. Here is one such time:

> *In the seventh month, in the one and twentieth day of the month, came the word of the Lord by the prophet Haggai, saying, Speak now to Zerubbabel the son of Shealtiel, governor of Judah, and to Joshua the son of Josedech, the high priest, and to the residue of the people, saying, Who is left among you that saw this house in her first glory? and how do ye see it now? is it not in your eyes in comparison of it as nothing? Yet now be strong, O Zerubbabel, saith the Lord; and be strong, O Joshua, son of Josedech, the high priest; and be strong, all ye people of the land, saith the Lord, and work: for I am with you, saith the Lord of hosts: According to the word*

that I covenanted with you when ye came out of Egypt, so my spirit remaineth among you: fear ye not. For thus saith the Lord of hosts; Yet once, it is a little while, and I will shake the heavens, and the earth, and the sea, and the dry land; And I will shake all nations, and the desire of all nations shall come: and I will fill this house with glory, saith the Lord of hosts. The silver is mine, and the gold is mine, saith the Lord of hosts. The glory of this latter house shall be greater than of the former, saith the Lord of hosts: and in this place will I give peace, saith the Lord of hosts (Haggai 2:1-9).

As it was with the temple, so is it with the church. The temple, the church, will be restored and the glory of it will exceed that of its past. This is that time God has set to restore His church; all that was we will be again—and greater! This is the time we have been waiting for, looking for, and praying for! Our time has come. The move of God is afoot.

Oh, the Suffering

What about the suffering? All the suffering was a part of the process. The suffering has produced the glory and prepared us for the coming shakeup, the separation.

A Time of Separation

See that ye refuse not him that speaketh. For if they escaped not who refused him that spake on earth, much more shall not we escape, if we turn away from him that speaketh from heaven: Whose voice then shook the earth: but now he hath promised, saying, Yet once more I shake

> *not the earth only, but also heaven. And this word, Yet once more, signifieth the removing of those things that are shaken, as of things that are made, that those things which cannot be shaken may remain* (Hebrews 12:25-27).

Who will be standing after the shaking?

> *Wherefore we receiving a kingdom which cannot be moved, let us have grace, whereby we may serve God acceptably with reverence and godly fear: For our God is a consuming fire (Hebrews 12:28-29).*

What happens once the separation is completed? It is time for us to say, as the apostle Paul said, "My preaching and teaching will not be just words of wisdom, but with power and demonstration by the spirit." For God will be God in the earth, and His name alone will be exalted! For the earth is the Lord's and the fullness thereof. He says, "I will restore, for this is the time of restoration." We are moving from suffering to glory. Get ready!

Tell yourself, "The suffering I have gone through has only prepared me for this time. I have been chosen by God for this season." This is the season of glory, and we are the ones it will be revealed through. This is the beginning of the last-day move of God. The glory that will be revealed is a demonstration of Holy Ghost power like the world has never seen. The greater works are here.

Tell yourself, "It's in me, and it's been building." For we have this treasure in earthen vessels that the excellency of the power may be of God and not of us. This is a necessary time. The help can only be released through the power of His glory, which is in us. We are a generation of royal priests who have been placed over the house of God to help in this time of need.

Called to Be a Witness

CHAPTER NINE

Kingdom Citizens, the Authority of the Kingdom, and Revealing the Kingdom

We are no more strangers but citizens of the kingdom of God. We must know who we are while we are on the earth.

And you hath he quickened, who were dead in trespasses and sins; Wherein in time past ye walked according to the course of this world, according to the prince of the power of the air, the spirit that now worketh in the children of disobedience: Among whom also we all had our conversation in times past in the lusts of our flesh, fulfilling the desires of the flesh and of the mind; and were by nature the children of wrath, even as others. But God, who is rich in mercy, for his great love wherewith he loved us, Even when we were dead in sins, hath quickened us together with Christ, (by grace ye are saved;) And hath raised us up together, and made us sit together in heavenly places in Christ Jesus: That in the ages to come he might shew the exceeding riches of his grace in his kindness toward us through Christ Jesus.

For by grace are ye saved through faith; and that not of yourselves: it is the gift of God: Not of works, lest any man should boast. For we are his workmanship, created in Christ Jesus unto good works, which God hath before ordained that we should walk in them. Wherefore remember, that ye being in time past Gentiles in the flesh, who are called Uncircumcision by that which is called the Circumcision in the flesh made by hands; That at that time ye were without Christ, being aliens from the commonwealth of Israel, and strangers from the covenants of promise, having no hope, and without God in the world: But now in Christ Jesus ye who sometimes were far off are made nigh by the blood of Christ.

For he is our peace, who hath made both one, and hath broken down the middle wall of partition between us; Having abolished in his flesh the enmity, even the law of commandments contained in ordinances; for to make in himself of twain one new man, so making peace; And that he might reconcile both unto God in one body by the cross, having slain the enmity thereby: And came and preached peace to you which were afar off, and to them that were nigh. For through him we both have access by one Spirit unto the Father. Now therefore ye are no more strangers and foreigners, but fellow citizens with the saints, and of the household of God; And are built upon the foundation of the apostles and prophets, Jesus Christ himself being the chief corner stone; In whom all the building fitly framed together groweth unto an holy temple in the Lord: In whom ye also are

> *builded together for an habitation of God through the Spirit* (Ephesians 2:1-22).

The kingdom is the kingdom of God. We are on the earth, but we are not citizens of the earth. Whenever someone becomes a citizen of another country,

- they must learn the rules and laws of the country;
- they acquire the rights of a citizen and the responsibility and benefits of citizenship; and
- an induction occurs where the individual denounces their allegiance to all others.

By being a citizen of heaven, we must denounce all other allegiances. While we are we stationed here on earth, we are ambassadors for the kingdom of God.

> *Therefore if any man be in Christ, he is a new creature: old things are passed away; behold, all things are become new. And all things are of God, who hath reconciled us to himself by Jesus Christ, and hath given to us the ministry of reconciliation; To wit, that God was in Christ, reconciling the world unto himself, not imputing their trespasses unto them; and hath committed unto us the word of reconciliation. Now then we are ambassadors for Christ, as though God did beseech you by us: we pray you in Christ's stead, be ye reconciled to God* (2 Corinthians 5:17-20).

The earth and its citizens are dying. It is our job to try to save as many as possible. We must be able to show them the benefits we have as citizens of the kingdom of God, so they can compare. There are many benefits of citizenship in the kingdom:

- We have a kingship. We have moved from death to life.
- We have been adopted into the royal family. We are children of the King.
- The limitations of the earth no longer apply to us, for we are part of a kingdom where all things are possible.

The King, who is our Father, loves us very much. We have been called to be witnesses of His kingdom and His goodness. We know the goodness of God leads men to repentance. Can the world look on us with the desire to have what we have?

We must walk in integrity because we are representing the King. We are joint heirs, co-owners—it is a family business. It is not just about getting saved and going to heaven. There is work that needs to be done. Do you realize that Sodom and Gomorrah could have been saved if just ten righteous could have been found?

Prepare for the Demonstration

> *And my speech and my preaching was not with enticing words of man's wisdom, but in demonstration of the Spirit and of power: That your faith should not stand in the wisdom of men, but in the power of God* (1 Corinthians 2:4-5).

There must be demonstrations of the power of the kingdom. The people's faith and trust need to be in God. Do you understand the ramifications of being a citizen of the kingdom of God? Anything that is not from heaven does not apply to us. We are not subject to this world; neither the things of this world. We only answer to the kingdom of God.

Church, we must let our lives be a witness for the kingdom. Jesus is soon to come, and our works need to be done. We are to take ownership of our citizenship. We have been called into the kingdom of God for such a time like this. There needs to be a difference between the clean and the unclean, faith and fear.

The call of Noah is upon the church. A storm is coming—get into the ark. Get out of the world and into the kingdom of God and be saved. It was Noah's responsibility to preach about the coming storm and to build a place for survival. Let us be a watchman for this generation.

The Authority of the Kingdom

One of the most important factors about who we are in relation to the kingdom is greatly misunderstood, and that is, "What does our authority cover?" Let's start at the beginning.

In Genesis 1, it says that God made us in His own image and likeness. He gave man dominion over *all* the earth. As you know, all that was lost in the fall of man, the first Adam. The Bible teaches that whoever you yield to or submit yourself to obey, you are the servants to the one you obey (Romans 6:16).

All of mankind became the servant to darkness and took on the nature of our master Satan, the rebel. We were placed under the sentence of sin and death. Not only did we lose the image and likeness of God, but also our authority over all the earth.

> *And the devil, taking him up into an high mountain, shewed unto him all the kingdoms of the world in a moment of time. And the devil said unto him, All this power will I give thee, and the glory of them: for that is delivered unto me; and to whomsoever I will I give it. If thou therefore wilt worship me, all shall be thine* (Luke 4:5-7).

As we read this passage, notice that Jesus did not question Satan's authority over the earth; He knew that mankind had lost it all. Man's body, mind, and soul was lost to Satan, and his authority over the earth was gone.

The Second Adam

We know that when the second Adam came, He restored all that was lost.

> *For since by man came death, by man came also the resurrection of the dead. For as in Adam all die, even so in Christ shall all be made alive. But every man in his own order: Christ the first fruits; afterward they that are Christ's at his coming. Then cometh the end, when he shall have delivered up the kingdom to God, even the Father; when he shall have put down all rule and all authority and power. For he must reign, till he hath put all enemies under his feet. The last enemy that shall be destroyed is death.*
>
> *But some man will say, How are the dead raised up? and with what body do they come? Thou fool, that which thou sowest is not quickened, except it die: And that which thou sowest, thou sowest not that body that shall be, but bare grain, it may chance of wheat, or of some*

> *other grain: But God giveth it a body as it hath pleased him, and to every seed his own body. All flesh is not the same flesh: but there is one kind of flesh of men, another flesh of beasts, another of fishes, and another of birds. There are also celestial bodies, and bodies terrestrial: but the glory of the celestial is one, and the glory of the terrestrial is another. There is one glory of the sun, and another glory of the moon, and another glory of the stars: for one star differeth from another star in glory.*
>
> *So also is the resurrection of the dead. It is sown in corruption; it is raised in incorruption: It is sown in dishonour; it is raised in glory: it is sown in weakness; it is raised in power: It is sown a natural body; it is raised a spiritual body. There is a natural body, and there is a spiritual body. And so it is written, The first man Adam was made a living soul; the last Adam was made a quickening spirit. Howbeit that was not first which is spiritual, but that which is natural; and afterward that which is spiritual. The first man is of the earth, earthy; the second man is the Lord from heaven. As is the earthy, such are they also that are earthy: and as is the heavenly, such are they also that are heavenly. And as we have borne the image of the earthy, we shall also bear the image of the heavenly* (1 Corinthians 15:21-26, 35-49).

We see that not only was the image restored, but all things were restored, including our authority. All this came along with our restored sonship. By the blood of Jesus, all our sin debt has been paid in full. Romans 8 tells us that everyone who receives Christ as their Lord and Savior no longer has any condemnation because they have been born of the Spirit. What does this all mean? Let's read.

But ye are not in the flesh, but in the Spirit, if so be that the Spirit of God dwell in you. Now if any man have not the Spirit of Christ, he is none of his. And if Christ be in you, the body is dead because of sin; but the Spirit is life because of righteousness. But if the Spirit of him that raised up Jesus from the dead dwell in you, he that raised up Christ from the dead shall also quicken your mortal bodies by his Spirit that dwelleth in you. Therefore, brethren, we are debtors, not to the flesh, to live after the flesh. For if ye live after the flesh, ye shall die: but if ye through the Spirit do mortify the deeds of the body, ye shall live. For as many as are led by the Spirit of God, they are the sons of God. For ye have not received the spirit of bondage again to fear; but ye have received the Spirit of adoption, whereby we cry, Abba, Father. The Spirit itself beareth witness with our spirit, that we are the children of God: And if children, then heirs; heirs of God, and joint-heirs with Christ; if so be that we suffer with him, that we may be also glorified together (Romans 8:9-17).

As the scripture explains, when you receive Christ and are born of the Spirit, you become joint-heirs with Him. This is the place where our authority and dominion was restored.

The Second Witness

Ephesians 1 explains that Christ was raised from the dead and was seated at the right hand of the Father. He is in the heavenly places, above all principalities, powers, dominions, and all names. The Holy Ghost bears us witness, for the Spirit of Jesus (the Son) has been sent, and now we have Holy Ghost power.

Remember what it says in Ephesians 6:12-13:

> *For we wrestle not against flesh and blood, but against principalities, against powers, against the rulers of the darkness of this world, against spiritual wickedness in high places. Wherefore take unto you the whole armour of God, that ye may be able to withstand in the evil day, and having done all, to stand.*

Church, it doesn't matter who Satan is and what he has rule over. His authority changed since Jesus, our elder brother, put him in his place! He gave us back our dominion in the earth.

> *And you hath he quickened, who were dead in trespasses and sins; Wherein in time past ye walked according to the course of this world, according to the prince of the power of the air, the spirit that now worketh in the children of disobedience: Among whom also we all had our conversation in times past in the lusts of our flesh, fulfilling the desires of the flesh and of the mind; and were by nature the children of wrath, even as others. But God, who is rich in mercy, for his great love wherewith he loved us, Even when we were dead in sins, hath quickened us together with Christ, (by grace ye are saved;) And hath raised us up together, and made us sit together in heavenly places in Christ Jesus: That in the ages to come he might shew the exceeding riches of his grace in his kindness toward us through Christ Jesus...For we are his workmanship, created in Christ Jesus unto good works, which God hath before ordained that we should walk in them* (Ephesians 2:1-7, 10).

The Power and Authority

Most don't understand that the power and authority of God is released through the structure of government. Wherever God has dominion, He sets up his government (His church), and that's where He operates. Everything that is in his dominion is blessed.

Ambassadors

The kingdom of God has come to conquer and establish colonies until once again, the whole is under its dominion. This is upon us—that is why God is reclaiming and restoring His church. We are governmental agents. Let's read:

> *Therefore if any man be in Christ, he is a new creature: old things are passed away; behold, all things are become new. And all things are of God, who hath reconciled us to himself by Jesus Christ, and hath given to us the ministry of reconciliation; To wit, that God was in Christ, reconciling the world unto himself, not imputing their trespasses unto them; and hath committed unto us the word of reconciliation. Now then we are ambassadors for Christ, as though God did beseech you by us: we pray you in Christ's stead, be ye reconciled to God* (2 Corinthians 5:17-20).

Imagine that—we speak for God. It may be hard to wrap your mind around it, but it's true. So how does the kingdom grow? I am glad you asked. We must remember, the kingdom was in Jesus, and everywhere He went He sowed seeds of the kingdom. Now it's our turn.

When Jesus was preparing His disciples to release them, part of their training was to go out and witness.

> *And the seventy returned again with joy, saying, Lord, even the devils are subject unto us through thy name. And he said unto them, I beheld Satan as lightning fall from heaven. Behold, I give unto you power to tread on serpents and scorpions, and over all the power of the enemy: and nothing shall by any means hurt you. Notwithstanding in this rejoice not, that the spirits are subject unto you; but rather rejoice, because your names are written in heaven* (Luke 10:17-20).

First let me digress. As you can see, this was not the twelve disciples, but seventy others. They were a part of the "whosoevers." The task of spreading seeds of the kingdom is not just for the five-fold ministers, but for the lay people as well.

As we just read, where we go, the kingdom goes with us to release seed and exercise authority over the present kingdom and its rulers, to gain new territory, to receive new citizens, and to set up colonies (fellowship) across the world.

Revealing the Kingdom

> *For the kingdom of God is not meat and drink; but righteousness, and peace, and joy in the Holy Ghost* (Romans 14:17).

We are living in a time of hopelessness, where people are suffering from so many things. They have been looking everywhere for help, just to come up empty. The help we all need can only be found in the kingdom of God. So it is our responsibility, as the church of the living God, to reveal the kingdom.

Before we can reveal the kingdom to others, the kingdom must first be revealed in us, and in order for that to take place, the transformation process must be completed. When we think of the kingdom, here are a few things that come to mind:

- Who is the King? Jesus
- What is His dominion? All creation
- How does one become a citizen? Born into it
- What are the benefits of citizenship? Access to all things pertaining to life and godliness and eternal life

The Son's Responsibility

As sons, we are to administer the help that the kingdom provides. Our biggest challenge is to make the invisible kingdom visible. One must be born into it in order to even see it. We must preach the gospel of the kingdom with power and demonstration in order for some to believe.

The Visible Kingdom Vs. the Invisible Kingdom

We all live in a physical world that has laws and restrictions that limit us, and it is not able to provide us with everything we need. In the invisible kingdom, however, all our needs are met and all things are possible.

In the invisible kingdom, we are not just citizens, we are family and have been made a part of the family business, *joint heirs.* What love and honor the King has bestowed upon us that we are called the sons of God and have been made joint heirs with Christ. Now we are a part of the royal priesthood and have been given power to loose and bind. That which was invisible has now been made visible through its citizens.

Listen, the help the world *needs* is in us. It is the seed, the word of God, which is God, and it has been transforming us. Church, it is our time; the kingdom of God is at hand. It is in us; now let us release it. There is a river in us that *needs* to flow out of us. There is help in the house. Say it out loud—there is help in God's house!

The transformation process is almost completed. Get ready, there is a fresh anointing in the house. There will be no more singing songs like *Please Be Patient With Me for God Is Not Through With Me Yet*—we will be changed!

Our preaching is not with enticing words of man's wisdom, but with power and demonstration by the Holy Spirit that your faith will not be in man, but in God.

There is help in the house!

To the Called: the Glory of the Latter House

CHAPTER TEN

We, the people of God, are the temple of God. In this time, we will see God restoring His temple. In the past, the temple was considered God's headquarters in the earth, His, and we were His ambassadors. We (the church) are the ones He was talking about when He said, "I will build my church."

> *When Jesus came into the coasts of Caesarea Philippi, he asked his disciples, saying, Whom do men say that I the Son of man am? And they said, Some say that thou art John the Baptist: some, Elias; and others, Jeremias, or one of the prophets. He saith unto them, But whom say ye that I am? And Simon Peter answered and said, Thou art the Christ, the Son of the living God. And Jesus answered and said unto him, Blessed art thou, Simon Barjona: for flesh and blood hath not revealed it unto thee, but my Father which is in heaven. And I say also unto thee, That thou art Peter, and upon this rock I will build my church; and the gates of hell shall not prevail against it. And I will give unto thee the keys of the kingdom of heaven: and whatsoever thou shalt bind on earth shall be bound in*

> *heaven: and whatsoever thou shalt loose on earth shall be loosed in heaven* (Matthew 16:13-19).

This is who we are supposed to be in the earth. As I said earlier, the church of our day has been compromised. We no longer walk in the anointing that was demonstrated in the book of Acts.

> *Now Peter and John went up together into the temple at the hour of prayer, being the ninth hour. And a certain man lame from his mother's womb was carried, whom they laid daily at the gate of the temple which is called Beautiful, to ask alms of them that entered into the temple; Who seeing Peter and John about to go into the temple asked an alms. And Peter, fastening his eyes upon him with John, said, Look on us. And he gave heed unto them, expecting to receive something of them. Then Peter said, Silver and gold have I none; but such as I have give I thee: In the name of Jesus Christ of Nazareth rise up and walk. And he took him by the right hand, and lifted him up: and immediately his feet and ankle bones received strength. And he leaping up stood, and walked, and entered with them into the temple, walking, and leaping, and praising God* (Acts 3:1-8).

This was an awesome thing. I wonder how many of us can say we are looked upon like that. There was a time in the Old Testament when the temple of God was torn down, and the next generation rebuilt it.

> *In the seventh month, in the one and twentieth day of the month, came the word of the Lord by the prophet Haggai, saying, Speak now to Zerubbabel the son of Shealtiel, governor of Judah, and to Joshua the son of*

> *Josedech, the high priest, and to the residue of the people, saying, Who is left among you that saw this house in her first glory? and how do ye see it now? is it not in your eyes in comparison of it as nothing?* (Haggai 2:1-3).

They were to compare the present temple with the former one, but there was no comparison. This is what was said about the latter temple.

> *For thus saith the Lord of hosts; Yet once, it is a little while, and I will shake the heavens, and the earth, and the sea, and the dry land; And I will shake all nations, and the desire of all nations shall come: and I will fill this house with glory, saith the Lord of hosts. The silver is mine, and the gold is mine, saith the Lord of hosts. The glory of this latter house shall be greater than of the former, saith the Lord of hosts: and in this place will I give peace, saith the Lord of hosts* (Haggai 2:6-9).

As you can see, Haggai was prophesying of the temple that was yet to be built in Israel. This was God's physical temple that Solomon built for his father David, which was to be built in the last days so that the sacrifices would once again commence.

Why was the temple down and the sacrifices discontinued? The sacrifices I am speaking of are those animal sacrifices that were once offered for the sins of the people but were no longer offered because there was no temple.

During this time, the perfect sacrifice came and was offered up on the tree, and that cleansed us from all sins. He became the foundation and the head of the church, His body. In this season, however, the church has lost most of its luster. It is simply not the same, but as Haggai prophesied, the latter temple of David would be built and its glory would exceed all the previous temples, and so will it be with the church—the temple that God built.

> *When Jesus came into the coasts of Caesarea Philippi, he asked his disciples, saying, Whom do men say that I the Son of man am? And they said, Some say that thou art John the Baptist: some, Elias; and others, Jeremias, or one of the prophets. He saith unto them, But whom say ye that I am? And Simon Peter answered and said, Thou art the Christ, the Son of the living God. And Jesus answered and said unto him, Blessed art thou, Simon Barjona: for flesh and blood hath not revealed it unto thee, but my Father which is in heaven. And I say also unto thee, That thou art Peter, and upon this rock I will build my church; and the gates of hell shall not prevail against it. And I will give unto thee the keys of the kingdom of heaven: and whatsoever thou shalt bind on earth shall be bound in heaven: and whatsoever thou shalt loose on earth shall be loosed in heaven* (Matthew 16:13-19).

As Haggai spoke about a shaking that was to come, so did the writer of Hebrews, who described the transition from the Levitical priesthood to Christ, the High Priest who abides forever over the house of God. He was preparing the church for its final push by walking in the greater glory.

> *For ye are not come unto the mount that might be touched, and that burned with fire, nor unto blackness, and darkness, and tempest, And the sound of a trumpet, and the voice of words; which voice they that heard intreated that the word should not be spoken to them any more: (For they could not endure that which was*

> *commanded, And if so much as a beast touch the mountain, it shall be stoned, or thrust through with a dart: And so terrible was the sight, that Moses said, I exceedingly fear and quake:) But ye are come unto mount Sion, and unto the city of the living God, the heavenly Jerusalem, and to an innumerable company of angels, To the general assembly and church of the firstborn, which are written in heaven, and to God the Judge of all, and to the spirits of just men made perfect, And to Jesus the mediator of the new covenant, and to the blood of sprinkling, that speaketh better things than that of Abel.*
>
> *See that ye refuse not him that speaketh. For if they escaped not who refused him that spake on earth, much more shall not we escape, if we turn away from him that speaketh from heaven: Whose voice then shook the earth: but now he hath promised, saying, Yet once more I shake not the earth only, but also heaven. And this word, Yet once more, signifieth the removing of those things that are shaken, as of things that are made, that those things which cannot be shaken may remain. Wherefore we receiving a kingdom which cannot be moved, let us have grace, whereby we may serve God acceptably with reverence and godly fear: For our God is a consuming fire* (Hebrews 12:18-29).

Haggai was told that he had everything that would be needed to rebuild the temple, and only silver and gold were to be used.

> *The silver is mine, and the gold is mine, saith the Lord of hosts. The glory of this latter house shall be greater than of the former, saith the Lord of hosts: and in this place will I give peace, saith the Lord of hosts* (Haggai 2:8-9).

The Bible talks about the harvest being great and the laborers being few; so again, the word to the called is, "It's our season." Let God complete the work in us, His temple, so the work can start. Look what God said was going on with His people and what He had to do:

> *Moreover the word of the Lord came unto me, saying, Son of man, when the house of Israel dwelt in their own land, they defiled it by their own way and by their doings: their way was before me as the uncleanness of a removed woman. Wherefore I poured my fury upon them for the blood that they had shed upon the land, and for their idols wherewith they had polluted it: And I scattered them among the heathen, and they were dispersed through the countries: according to their way and according to their doings I judged them. And when they entered unto the heathen, whither they went, they profaned my holy name, when they said to them, These are the people of the Lord, and are gone forth out of his land. But I had pity for mine holy name, which the house of Israel had profaned among the heathen, whither they went.*
>
> *Therefore say unto the house of Israel, thus saith the Lord God; I do not this for your sakes, O house of Israel, but for mine holy name's sake, which ye have profaned among the heathen, whither ye went. And I will sanctify my great name, which was profaned among the heathen, which ye have profaned in the midst of them; and the heathen shall know that I am the Lord, saith the Lord God, when I shall be sanctified in you before their eyes. For I will take you from among the heathen, and gather you out of all countries, and will bring you into your own land. Then will I sprinkle clean water upon you, and ye*

shall be clean: from all your filthiness, and from all your idols, will I cleanse you. A new heart also will I give you, and a new spirit will I put within you: and I will take away the stony heart out of your flesh, and I will give you an heart of flesh. And I will put my spirit within you, and cause you to walk in my statutes, and ye shall keep my judgments, and do them. And ye shall dwell in the land that I gave to your fathers; and ye shall be my people, and I will be your God (Ezekiel 36:16-28).

It's all about what God is doing for His great name's sake. Now we can understand Jude a little better—how he challenged the people to seek that which was because it's ours. God gave it to us, and now He is restoring it to us.

Beloved, when I gave all diligence to write unto you of the common salvation, it was needful for me to write unto you, and exhort you that ye should earnestly contend for the faith which was once delivered unto the saints...But ye, beloved, building up yourselves on your most holy faith, praying in the Holy Ghost (Jude 3, 20).

We have been told to not get weary in doing well, for in due season we will reap if we do not faint. Don't settle for what you have or where you are. There is more, much more, and God is doing it because of His great name. During this season, we must know the voice of God, so that He might lead us to fulfill His purpose for us.

Beloved, believe not every spirit, but try the spirits whether they are of God: because many false prophets are gone out into the world (1 John 4:1).

There are many spirits in the world, and each has a voice. They are all speaking to humanity for the purpose of influencing or controlling. They are manifesting themselves in mankind.

The Disguises

Satan was the angel of light. His name means "to deceive." Satan is a deceiver, which leads us to the subject of knowing God's voice.

As you can see, with so many voices speaking, the question I must ask is, "Can you recognize *God's voice* above all else?" The word *recognize* means able to identify.

We all know that to be able to identify a person by voice, we must know them *well* and we must know them *personally*.

I am finding that in order for many of us to find rest, we must first be comforted. Sometimes we can be comforted by others, but there comes a time when only a word from God will suffice. This is the season, for all this is, for our working purpose. Let me explain: there is a collective purpose or function and there is a personal function.

In order for us to accomplish God's purpose in our lives, we must be able to recognize God's voice. If He speaks directly or through others, we must know it's God. 1 Kings 19 gives us an example of knowing God's voice:

> *And Ahab told Jezebel all that Elijah had done, and withal how he had slain all the prophets with the sword. Then Jezebel sent a messenger unto Elijah, saying, So let the gods do to me, and more also, if I make not thy life as the life of one of them by to morrow about this time. And when he saw that, he arose, and went for his life, and came to Beersheba, which belongeth to Judah, and left his servant there. But he himself went a day's journey into the*

wilderness, and came and sat down under a juniper tree: and he requested for himself that he might die; and said, It is enough; now, O Lord, take away my life; for I am not better than my fathers. And as he lay and slept under a juniper tree, behold, then an angel touched him, and said unto him, Arise and eat. And he looked, and, behold, there was a cake baken on the coals, and a cruse of water at his head. And he did eat and drink, and laid him down again. And the angel of the Lord came again the second time, and touched him, and said, Arise and eat; because the journey is too great for thee. And he arose, and did eat and drink, and went in the strength of that meat forty days and forty nights unto Horeb the mount of God.

And he came thither unto a cave, and lodged there; and, behold, the word of theLord came to him, and he said unto him, What doest thou here, Elijah? And he said, I have been very jealous for the Lord God of hosts: for the children of Israel have forsaken thy covenant, thrown down thine altars, and slain thy prophets with the sword; and I, even I only, am left; and they seek my life, to take it away. And he said, Go forth, and stand upon the mount before the Lord. And, behold, the Lord passed by, and a great and strong wind rent the mountains, and brake in pieces the rocks before the Lord; but the Lord was not in the wind: and after the wind an earthquake; but the Lord was not in the earthquake: And after the earthquake a fire; but the Lord was not in the fire: and after the fire a still small voice (1 Kings 19:1-12).

When we are operating corporately as a body, recognizing the voice of God falls mainly on the leaders. There will be times when we are on a mission by God or we have been placed in a situation by God, and now we are waiting for further instructions. Satan has been looking for a chance to mislead us. We are all going through and looking for a word.

I have found that sometimes, a person can be speaking in general and God will give them a word without them knowing it.

However, the word I am talking about is a word directly from God to us. We need this training for the work that lies ahead.

> *And it came to pass after these things, that God did tempt Abraham, and said unto him, Abraham: and he said, Behold, here I am. And he said, Take now thy son, thine only son Isaac, whom thou lovest, and get thee into the land of Moriah; and offer him there for a burnt offering upon one of the mountains which I will tell thee of. And Abraham rose up early in the morning, and saddled his ass, and took two of his young men with him, and Isaac his son, and clave the wood for the burnt offering, and rose up, and went unto the place of which God had told him* (Genesis 22:1-3).

If this had been you, what would you have been thinking by now? Most probably you would be saying, "The devil is a liar, and I rebuke you!" Church, we must be able to recognize God's voice so that when the instructions don't make sense, we can still obey. Other examples include Peter on the water, the widow's last cake, Hosea taking on a prostitute for a wife, and the list goes on and on.

It reminds me of when my wife and I went to purchase our first new car. At first, we were rejected, but God sent us back a second time to the same place. This time, we were approved and the car was ours.

Another time, my wife was told that she needed an operation or she would die. The doctors were certain that she needed this surgery and had everything prepared. The Lord spoke to her as she lay in the hospital and told her she didn't need the operation. He spoke to me while I was at home and told me He was going to heal her. Long story short, He did just that. He healed her body without the surgery.

I believe that the world is going to see fantastic things done by God through us, and we must be ready for it. Say to yourselves, "Signs and wonders! My Father is the God of signs and wonders, and I am a chip off the old block." Our Father works, and we also work.

You are probably saying, "Look at me, I am not worthy or qualified." Neither was Peter; he denied knowing Christ three times. Gideon was called a mighty man of valor. God is not surprised—He knows who you are.

Hope in everything else is failing, so we must become the hope. This is our season to be revealed, but we must know the *voice* of God so that we can obey. For He declares in His word, "My sheep know My voice and a stranger they will not follow." If that is so, then follow.

Our Present Help

CHAPTER ELEVEN

God was saying to me in my prayer time that He is a *right-now* God. To the called, God is saying He is our present help. He is not just the God of the past nor just the God of the future. We must understand that He is also the God of the present. He is here to help us with our needs and with the work.

He Says

History is good, it was written so that you can learn about Me, to know My ways, but you are not to live in the past. It's time to know Me in the present.

So, people, this is not about history, this is about what God is saying and doing *now*. So what are His plans? Can we know them? The answer is yes!

Howbeit we speak wisdom among them that are perfect: yet not the wisdom of this world, nor of the princes of this world, that come to nought: But we speak the wisdom of God in a mystery, even the hidden wisdom, which God ordained before the world unto our glory: Which none of the princes of this world knew: for had they known it, they would not have crucified the Lord of glory. But as it is written, Eye hath not seen, nor ear heard, neither have entered into the heart of man, the things which God hath prepared for them that love him. But God hath revealed them unto us by his Spirit: for the Spirit searcheth all things, yea, the deep things of God. For what man knoweth the things of a man, save the spirit of man which is in him? even so the things of God knoweth no man, but the Spirit of God.

Now we have received, not the spirit of the world, but the spirit which is of God; that we might know the things that are freely given to us of God. Which things also we speak, not in the words which man's wisdom teacheth, but which the Holy Ghost teacheth; comparing spiritual things with spiritual. But the natural man receiveth not the things of the Spirit of God: for they are foolishness unto him: neither can he know them, because they are spiritually discerned. But he that is spiritual judgeth all things, yet he himself is judged of no man. For who hath known the mind of the Lord, that he may instruct him? but we have the mind of Christ (1 Corinthians 2:6-16).

It's God's word that says it, not me!

His Plans

First of all, God is taking His church back. He says,

For too long, My church (My body) has been controlled by man, ungodly men who have rendered Me disabled

> *and powerless. You must realize I live in you and work through My body, but its members have been compromised and have chosen to work independent of each other. So I have become handicapped in the earth.*

So the first order of business is to be restored. I *need* to be made whole again, so I can do my job. So right now, He is saying His plan is to restore His church and get it ready to be revealed.

Her Assignment

The assignment of the body, the church, is to reap His harvest!

> *Then saith he unto his disciples, The harvest truly is plenteous, but the labourers are few; Pray ye therefore the Lord of the harvest, that he will send forth labourers into his harvest* (Matthew 9:37-38).

People, the time is up for being consumed with one's self. Are you saved? If the answer is yes, then you will be just fine. You must not let the cares of life distract you from your purpose. Remember what was said in Matthew 6:25-26, 33:

> *Therefore I say unto you, Take no thought for your life, what ye shall eat, or what ye shall drink; nor yet for your body, what ye shall put on. Is not the life more than meat, and the body than raiment? Behold the fowls of the air: for they sow not, neither do they reap, nor gather into barns; yet your heavenly Father feedeth them. Are ye not much better than they?...But seek ye first the kingdom of God, and his righteousness; and all these things shall be added unto you.*

Understand, He has given us all things that pertain to life and godliness. So don't become caught up in worrying about things.

Our Focus

Instead of "woe is me," what we should really be thinking about is the lost souls. Shall we just let them be destroyed when we have been given power to help? We can help if we stop fighting one another long enough.

God's plan is to reap a harvest. So He is still asking us the same question He asked Isaiah in Isaiah 6:8-11.

> *Also I heard the voice of the Lord, saying, Whom shall I send, and who will go for us? Then said I, Here am I; send me. And he said, Go, and tell this people, Hear ye indeed, but understand not; and see ye indeed, but perceive not. Make the heart of this people fat, and make their ears heavy, and shut their eyes; lest they see with their eyes, and hear with their ears, and understand with their heart, and convert, and be healed. Then said I, Lord, how long? And he answered, Until the cities be wasted without inhabitant, and the houses without man, and the land be utterly desolate.*

People, God is on the move, for He is a right-now God. The good thing about this is that He is our present help. With or without us, the job will get done, so let's lay aside every weight of sin that can distract us and let us run with patience. He is our help so we can be a help. He has said, *"I will build my church, and the gates of hell shall not prevail against it."*

We have been called to set the captives free! To the called, He is still our present help.

It's in the House

The Lord has shown me that when the church learns how to be one and to understand that there's only one body, then they will recognize that all their help is in the house. So why do we bypass the body and go directly to God for our needs, when He has placed in the body gifts to help ourselves with?

There is no work outside of the body, no calling, no vision, no power, no victory, and no nothing without the body. We all are, or none of us are, because we are one.

> *Simon Peter, a servant and an apostle of Jesus Christ, to them that have obtained like precious faith with us through the righteousness of God and our Saviour Jesus Christ: Grace and peace be multiplied unto you through the knowledge of God, and of Jesus our Lord, According as his divine power hath given unto us all things that pertain unto life and godliness, through the knowledge of him that hath called us to glory and virtue* (2 Peter 1:1-3).

> *Now concerning spiritual gifts, brethren, I would not have you ignorant...Now there are diversities of gifts, but the same Spirit. And there are differences of administrations, but the same Lord. And there are diversities of operations, but it is the same God which worketh all in all. But the manifestation of the Spirit is given to every man to profit withal. For to one is given by the Spirit the word of wisdom; to another the word of knowledge by the same Spirit; To another faith by the same Spirit; to another the gifts of healing by the same Spirit; To another the working of miracles; to another*

prophecy; to another discerning of spirits; to another divers kinds of tongues; to another the interpretation of tongues: But all these worketh that one and the selfsame Spirit, dividing to every man severally as he will. For as the body is one, and hath many members, and all the members of that one body, being many, are one body: so also is Christ (1 Corinthians 12:1, 4-12).

I therefore, the prisoner of the Lord, beseech you that ye walk worthy of the vocation wherewith ye are called, With all lowliness and meekness, with longsuffering, forbearing one another in love; Endeavouring to keep the unity of the Spirit in the bond of peace...But unto every one of us is given grace according to the measure of the gift of Christ. Wherefore he saith, When he ascended up on high, he led captivity captive, and gave gifts unto men. (Now that he ascended, what is it but that he also descended first into the lower parts of the earth? He that descended is the same also that ascended up far above all heavens, that he might fill all things.) And he gave some, apostles; and some, prophets; and some, evangelists; and some, pastors and teachers; For the perfecting of the saints, for the work of the ministry, for the edifying of the body of Christ: Till we all come in the unity of the faith, and of the knowledge of the Son of God, unto a perfect man, unto the measure of the stature of the fulness of Christ...But speaking the truth in love, may grow up into him in all things, which is the head, even Christ: From whom the whole body fitly joined together and compacted by that which every joint supplieth, according to the effectual working in the measure of every part, maketh increase of the body unto the edifying of itself in love (Ephesians 4:1-3, 7-13, 15-16).

> *For he that eateth and drinketh unworthily, eateth and drinketh damnation to himself, not discerning the Lord's body. For this cause many are weak and sickly among you, and many sleep* (1 Corinthians 11:29-30).

We are weak and sickly because we are not discerning the body. Respect its members. Why would God put the help we need in the body and then let us ignore it? He doesn't—this is why so many in the church are suffering because first, they don't work to become one, and second, they have no covering.

In a natural body, there are abilities built in by God so it can heal itself, but there must be a connection. With the nation of Israel, they became very dry and lifeless because of a disconnect. Let's read:

> *The hand of the Lord was upon me, and carried me out in the spirit of the Lord, and set me down in the midst of the valley which was full of bones, And caused me to pass by them round about: and, behold, there were very many in the open valley; and, lo, they were very dry. And he said unto me, Son of man, can these bones live? And I answered, O Lord God, thou knowest...Then he said unto me, Son of man, these bones are the whole house of Israel: behold, they say, our bones are dried, and our hope is lost: we are cut off for our parts* (Ezekiel 37:1-3, 11).

God has made it impossible for us to live without one another. We are forced to get along and become one—the members and the head. A head without a body or a body without a head or a member without a body is *useless.*

Now we can understand the verse, *"A house divided against itself cannot stand."* If God has given us all things pertaining to life and godliness and placed them in the body, no wonder Satan is working overtime to bring disconnect. We will suffer much and die without a connection. We are never going to get what we need if we don't stay connected because it's all in the house. Usually, the hardest place to get connected and stay connected is the place God has purposed for us.

> *For by one Spirit are we all baptized into one body, whether we be Jews or Gentiles, whether we be bond or free; and have been all made to drink into one Spirit. For the body is not one member, but many. If the foot shall say, Because I am not the hand, I am not of the body; is it therefore not of the body? And if the ear shall say, Because I am not the eye, I am not of the body; is it therefore not of the body? If the whole body were an eye, where were the hearing? If the whole were hearing, where were the smelling? But now hath God set the members every one of them in the body, as it hath pleased him. And if they were all one member, where were the body? But now are they many members, yet but one body.*
>
> *And the eye cannot say unto the hand, I have no need of thee: nor again the head to the feet, I have no need of you. Nay, much more those members of the body, which seem to be more feeble, are necessary: And those members of the body, which we think to be less honourable, upon these we bestow more abundant honour; and our uncomely parts have more abundant comeliness. For our comely parts have no need: but God hath tempered the body together, having given more abundant honour to that part which lacked. That there should be no schism in the body; but that the members should have the same care one for another. And whether*

> *one member suffer, all the members suffer with it; or one member be honoured, all the members rejoice with it* (1 Corinthians 12:13-26).

Again, the points to remember are these:

1. We need one another.

2. Our help is in the house (body).

Church, the help is automatically released throughout the whole body simply by being connected.

> *And he gave some, apostles; and some, prophets; and some, evangelists; and some, pastors and teachers; For the perfecting of the saints, for the work of the ministry, for the edifying of the body of Christ: Till we all come in the unity of the faith, and of the knowledge of the Son of God, unto a perfect man, unto the measure of the stature of the fulness of Christ: That we henceforth be no more children, tossed to and fro, and carried about with every wind of doctrine, by the sleight of men, and cunning craftiness, whereby they lie in wait to deceive; But speaking the truth in love, may grow up into him in all things, which is the head, even Christ: From whom the whole body fitly joined together and compacted by that which every joint supplieth, according to the effectual working in the measure of every part, maketh increase of the body unto the edifying of itself in love* (Ephesians 4:11-16).

So let us love one another because what we need is already in the house (the body). *It is in the house!*

Where There is No Vision

CHAPTER TWELVE

It is so necessary for us to be able to see and know the will of God. This is critical in the dispensation of the church age. God has always had a plan of total redemption. The church has a great part to play in it, but as I said before, by the time the twentieth century rolled around, much of what the church was had been lost. By the time my generation (the baby boomers) came along, the church was just a shell of itself.

She has become compromised by her ungodly leaders. Many organized churches lost their integrity, respect, and anointing, including the Catholics. We all are made poorer because of it.

No Vision

History teaches that whenever things became dark, God would send light. People, the darkness is upon us, and we, the church, are the light that God is sending. All the things that we have talked about in this book are preparation for the very hour. I hope we have learned them well.

Zeal for the Work

It doesn't matter how zealous we are for the works of God; we are going nowhere unless God gives us insight into His plan. This leads me into this next chapter, Where There Is No Vision.

> *Where there is no vision, the people perish* (Proverbs 29:18).

Vision is the ability to see or to have sight. There are two sources of sight:

- our two eyes, and
- the ability to imagine or foresee, to create vision in the mind's eye.

Hopelessness is caused by short sightedness. If our sight is limited to the physical realm only, we will be miserable.

Spiritual Sight

It is necessary for us to develop spiritual sight. Why? If not, we will be caught unaware.

> *Let brotherly love continue. Be not forgetful to entertain strangers: for thereby some have entertained angels unawares. Remember them that are in bonds, as bound with them; and them which suffer adversity, as being yourselves also in the body* (Hebrews 13:1-3).

The word *unaware* means not knowing, not noticing, not expecting, or taken by surprise. The Lord is saying that we must keep ourselves built up and up to date in the

Spirit. We must be gifted with the ability to discern. There is danger all around us, and so many are not aware of it. There are tactics and schemes that Satan is using that are stealthy, undetected by the natural man.

We know that the fleshly (natural) man is unable to see into the spiritual realm and will be a victim to a stealth attack. When a weapon is being formed against him, by the time it is revealed to the natural man, it's too late. There are snares and entrapments that await us all. We must understand that the snares that are being made are made according to our weaknesses or vulnerabilities.

Example: Samson

As you know, before the birth of Samson, he was chosen to be a Nazarite, a deliverer of the people. When he became a man, he went about destroying Israel's enemies and no one could stop him. All the lords of the Philistines came together to plan how to stop Samson. Let's read:

> *And it came to pass afterward, that he loved a woman in the valley of Sorek, whose name was Delilah. And the lords of the Philistines came up unto her, and said unto her, Entice him, and see wherein his great strength lieth, and by what means we may prevail against him, that we may bind him to afflict him; and we will give thee every one of us eleven hundred pieces of silver. And Delilah said to Samson, Tell me, I pray thee, wherein thy great strength lieth, and wherewith thou mightest be bound to afflict thee. And Samson said unto her, If they bind me with seven green withs that were never dried, then shall I be weak, and be as another man.*

> *And it came to pass, when she pressed him daily with her words, and urged him, so that his soul was vexed unto death; That he told her all his heart, and said unto her, There hath not come a razor upon mine head; for I have been a Nazarite unto God from my mother's womb: if I be shaven, then my strength will go from me, and I shall become weak, and be like any other man. And when Delilah saw that he had told her all his heart, she sent and called for the lords of the Philistines, saying, Come up this once, for he hath shewed me all his heart. Then the lords of the Philistines came up unto her, and brought money in their hand. And she made him sleep upon her knees; and she called for a man, and she caused him to shave off the seven locks of his head; and she began to afflict him, and his strength went from him. And she said, The Philistines be upon thee, Samson. And he awoke out of his sleep, and said, I will go out as at other times before, and shake myself. And he wist not that the Lord was departed from him* (Judges 16:4-7, 16-20).

As you can see, the weapon was a woman. The sad part is, Samson did not know that he had lost his strength until it was too late. The weapon that Satan is targeting you with may not be that obvious. It could be as simple as a decision, an act of logic.

Many souls will be destroyed and lost, unaware. Church, sheep are very vulnerable. It's not their nature to be cognizant of their surroundings. Their focus is eating and reproducing. It is the shepherd's responsibility to lead them to new pastures and protect them.

Danger Ahead

Why? Many sheep have no shepherd, and many do not seek counsel before action. They have forgotten that the pastors are watchmen for the souls of the sheep. The Bible tell us of dangerous times ahead, and I don't want to see you being a victim of it. Church, we must be aware of the times in which we are living and the closeness of the coming of the Lord. Let's read:

> *And take heed to yourselves, lest at any time your hearts be overcharged with surfeiting, and drunkenness, and cares of this life, and so that day come upon you unawares. For as a snare shall it come on all them that dwell on the face of the whole earth. Watch ye therefore, and pray always, that ye may be accounted worthy to escape all these things that shall come to pass, and to stand before the Son of man* (Luke 21:34-36).

Let's look at the context:

> *And there shall be signs in the sun, and in the moon, and in the stars; and upon the earth distress of nations, with perplexity; the sea and the waves roaring; Men's hearts failing them for fear, and for looking after those things which are coming on the earth: for the powers of heaven shall be shaken. And then shall they see the Son of man coming in a cloud with power and great glory. And when these things begin to come to pass, then look up, and lift up your heads; for your redemption draweth nigh* (Luke 21:25-28).

For a little more clarity, let's read:

For as the lightning cometh out of the east, and shineth even unto the west; so shall also the coming of the Son of man be. For wheresoever the carcase is, there will the eagles be gathered together. Immediately after the tribulation of those days shall the sun be darkened, and the moon shall not give her light, and the stars shall fall from heaven, and the powers of the heavens shall be shaken: And then shall appear the sign of the Son of man in heaven: and then shall all the tribes of the earth mourn, and they shall see the Son of man coming in the clouds of heaven with power and great glory. And he shall send his angels with a great sound of a trumpet, and they shall gather together his elect from the four winds, from one end of heaven to the other (Matthew 24:27-31).

Now let's return to Luke:

And he spake to them a parable; Behold the fig tree, and all the trees; When they now shoot forth, ye see and know of your own selves that summer is now nigh at hand. So likewise ye, when ye see these things come to pass, know ye that the kingdom of God is nigh at hand. Verily I say unto you, This generation shall not pass away, till all be fulfilled. Heaven and earth shall pass away: but my words shall not pass away (Luke 21:29-33).

People, we have access to the gift of discernment; just ask the Holy Ghost, He is our guide. Church, these are the last days. Let's not get caught unaware. In the *will* or the promises of God, many things have been deeded to His people that we are not yet walking in. How shall we have hope for them? We must understand that the things of God are revealed to us not through intellect (teaching resources), but by the Spirit.

But as it is written, Eye hath not seen, nor ear heard, neither have entered into the heart of man, the things which God hath prepared for them that love him. But God hath revealed them unto us by his Spirit: for the Spirit searcheth all things, yea, the deep things of God. For what man knoweth the things of a man, save the spirit of man which is in him? even so the things of God knoweth no man, but the Spirit of God. Now we have received, not the spirit of the world, but the spirit which is of God; that we might know the things that are freely given to us of God (1 Corinthians 2:9-12).

People, for the most part we walk by faith. What is faith? It is the *substance* of things hoped for, and the evidence of things *not seen*. But occasionally it's good to see. Can you believe what you see by an awesome God? What did Thomas say when they told him that Jesus was alive?

King David took a different approach. Look what he said:

I had fainted, unless I had believed to see the goodness of the Lord in the land of the living (Psalm 27:13).

In some conditions, unless we can see into the spiritual realm (the eternal), we will not have hope in time. Remember the angel that visited Gideon? He called him a mighty man of valor. People, there are dangers and blessings that cannot be seen with our natural eyes.

Example of Blindness

Then the Lord opened the eyes of Balaam, and he saw the angel of the Lord standing in the way, and his sword

> *drawn in his hand: and he bowed down his head, and fell flat on his face. And the angel of the Lord said unto him, Wherefore hast thou smitten thine ass these three times? behold, I went out to withstand thee, because thy way is perverse before me: And the ass saw me, and turned from me these three times: unless she had turned from me, surely now also I had slain thee, and saved her alive. And Balaam said unto the angel of the Lord, I have sinned; for I knew not that thou stoodest in the way against me: now therefore, if it displease thee, I will get me back again. And the angel of the Lord said unto Balaam, Go with the men: but only the word that I shall speak unto thee, that thou shalt speak. So Balaam went with the princes of Balak.*
>
> *And when Balak heard that Balaam was come, he went out to meet him unto a city of Moab, which is in the border of Arnon, which is in the utmost coast. And Balak said unto Balaam, Did I not earnestly send unto thee to call thee? wherefore camest thou not unto me? am I not able indeed to promote thee to honour? And Balaam said unto Balak, Lo, I am come unto thee: have I now any power at all to say any thing? the word that God putteth in my mouth, that shall I speak. And Balaam went with Balak, and they came unto Kirjathhuzoth. And Balak offered oxen and sheep, and sent to Balaam, and to the princes that were with him. And it came to pass on the morrow, that Balak took Balaam, and brought him up into the high places of Baal, that thence he might see the utmost part of the people* (Numbers 22:31-41).

We need to understand that Satan controls and manipulates the physical realm to his own advantage, except for the territory claimed by God's people. This is why we need to know and see God's promises. Again, where there is blindness, the people perish.

> *Then the king of Syria warred against Israel, and took counsel with his servants, saying, In such and such a place shall be my camp. And the man of God sent unto the king of Israel, saying, Beware that thou pass not such a place; for thither the Syrians are come down. And the king of Israel sent to the place which the man of God told him and warned him of, and saved himself there, not once nor twice. Therefore the heart of the king of Syria was sore troubled for this thing; and he called his servants, and said unto them, Will ye not shew me which of us is for the king of Israel? And one of his servants said, None, my lord, O king: but Elisha, the prophet that is in Israel, telleth the king of Israel the words that thou speakest in thy bedchamber.*
>
> *And he said, Go and spy where he is, that I may send and fetch him. And it was told him, saying, Behold, he is in Dothan. Therefore sent he thither horses, and chariots, and a great host: and they came by night, and compassed the city about. And when the servant of the man of God was risen early, and gone forth, behold, an host compassed the city both with horses and chariots. And his servant said unto him, Alas, my master! how shall we do? And he answered, Fear not: for they that be with us are more than they that be with them. And Elisha prayed, and said, Lord, I pray thee, open his eyes, that he may see. And the Lord opened the eyes of the young man; and he saw: and, behold, the mountain was full of horses and chariots of fire round about Elisha* (2 Kings 6:8-17).

As you can see in this scripture, not everybody in the church can see. We must be in a right relationship with God for the Holy Ghost to reveal the spiritual realm to us. Church, we must be able to see beyond our conditions and situations.

There is always help. The question is, can you see it?

Mission Accomplished

CHAPTER THIRTEEN

In the previous twelve chapters, we have talked about many things the Lord is challenging us in to prepare us for the last days' kingdom work. We have things to do in order to be compliant, but for the most part, it will be God who is doing the work.

We are just His vessels that He has chosen before the foundation of the world. We were chosen. I know here in time, things look uncertain, but I can assure you that in God's plan, in eternity, everything is finished. So the last words I would like to impart are *mission accomplished.*

To the called, as the time of Jesus's arrival gets closer, there will be a great awakening in the very hearts of God's people that will cause a hunger in our very souls, like an unquenchable thirst. There will be those who will seek after the old landmarks, the place of holiness. It will be a time when those who had much will not have anything left over and those who have little or nothing will not go lacking. For we will have all things common. All things that would separate and divide us will be done away with. We will stand as one man with one voice, declaring the greatness of our God.

Then it will come to pass once again the psalm of King David:

> *I will bless the Lord at all times: his praise shall continually be in my mouth. My soul shall make her boast in the Lord: the humble shall hear thereof, and be glad. O magnify the Lord with me, and let us exalt his name together* (Psalm 34:1-3).

Our hearts will be made rich in His manifested glory. Our souls will be satisfied. Then no longer will we hunger or thirst for that for which we were born (our purpose) has finally been realized. All the earth will rejoice when we, the sons of God, are revealed. Again, it does not yet appear what we shall be, but we shall be like Him in all things.

To the called, this will be our finest hour. For Christ has made us to be His glorious church—a called-out people, ones who have been washed by His blood, empowered by His Spirit, and set as an arrow to the target called purpose, which is the right calling of God.

We are not to be weary or become faint, but just wait on the Lord—our strength will be renewed, and no weapon that tries to stop us shall succeed. We are called of the Lord and have been set in this time in history to destroy the works of the devil and to make desolate his kingdom, and to that end we will succeed.

The power of God shall be revealed through us as a flow, as a mighty river that covers the whole earth. Those who were once far off shall be drawn near, for the power of demonstration shall be so great that chains shall be broken and shackles shall fall, loosening the captive. The prison door shall swing open, and all shall be free to choose.

By the Spirit, I see the prophets of this generation stand up on their watch, lift their voices, and cry aloud. Behold, the bridegroom cometh; from the four corners of the earth, you can see the bride coming, decked in flowing white linen, pure in nature. The bridegroom stretches forth his hand and says, "Come, for all things are ready."

Then once again my eyes were cast toward the earth, and I saw a great field with a harvest ready to be gathered, and the Lord of the harvest said, "The harvest is mighty but the laborers are few." He turned and beckoned to recently released captives, for now it was the very last hour. As I was looking, the fields was flooded with workers and the harvest was saved.

Now the Lord said to the called, "I have now reaped what I have sown." A song was given as the harvest began to sing, for the harvest was the souls of a great multitude, and the song was, "We have been redeemed."

To the called, did I not tell you that I would build My church and the gates of hell would not prevail against her? I give to you the keys of the kingdom and whatever you loose on earth I will loose in heaven, and whatever you bind on earth I will bind in heaven. Only be not afraid. That which I have spoken I will do. Be strong, I will not fail you, nor will I forsake you, for the mouth of the Lord has spoken it.

To the called,

> *The grace of our Lord Jesus Christ be with you all. Amen. Now to him that is of power to stablish you according to my gospel, and the preaching of Jesus Christ, according to the revelation of the mystery, which was kept secret since the world began, But now is made manifest, and by the scriptures of the prophets,*

according to the commandment of the everlasting God, made known to all nations for the obedience of faith: To God only wise, be glory through Jesus Christ for ever. Amen (Romans 16:24-27).

www.ingramcontent.com/pod-product-compliance
Ingram Content Group UK Ltd.
Pitfield, Milton Keynes, MK11 3LW, UK
UKHW020226250726
13967UKWH00001B/213